let's speak JAPANESE

MANUAL FOR CONVERSATIONAL JAPANESE

BY YOSHIYUKI KAWATA

ILLUSTRATIONS & COVER DESIGN
by
MARK WATERS

All rights reserved. No part of this book may be reproduced or transmitted in any form or by any means, electronic or mechanical, including photocopying, recording or by any information storage and retrieval system, without written permission in writing from the Publisher.

Copyright 1977.

THE PETROGLYPH PRESS, LTD.
201 Kinoole Street
Hilo, Hawaii 96720

ISBN 0-912180-29-3

First published in the United States in 1977
Eighth Printing - August 1991

CONTENTS

		page
Preface		7
Lesson 1	"Doko e ikimasu ka."	9
Lesson 2	"Doko de hon o kaimasu ka."	15
Lesson 3	"Daigaku wa doko ni arimasu ka." "Sensei wa doko ni imasu ka."	23
Lesson 4	"Mada kimasen yo."	31
Lesson 5	"Are wa nan desu ka."	39
Lesson 6	"Supootsu ga suki desu ka."	45
Lesson 7	"Honda ja arimasen."	53
Lesson 8	"Totemo omoshirokatta desu yo."	61
Lesson 9	Supiichi	67
Lesson 10	"Donna nyuusu deshita ka."	75
Lesson 11	"Sochira no wa o-ikura desu ka."	83

Useful Expressions (1) ... 89
Useful Expressions (2) ... 90
Useful Expressions (3) ... 91
Chart of Adjectives ... 92
Pattern Sentences of Adjectives ... 95
Chart of Noun-Adjectives ... 96
Pattern Sentences of Noun-Adjectives ... 98
Verb Chart ... 99
Pattern Sentences of Verbs
    (1) Vowel Verbs ... 100
    (2) Consonant Verbs ... 101
    (3) Irregular Verb, "Kuru" ... 103
    (4) Irregular Verb, "Suru" ... 104

TO MY MOTHER, YAE TAKAHASHI

PREFACE

To master a foreign language is not an easy task. Acquaintance with the language, however, enhances one's rapport with the language speaking people, as they find friendliness in the effort one has been making to communicate with or understand them. Language has a fantastic power, indeed, to bring people closer.

The language cannot be learned with disregard of the culture of the people which closely relates to the language they speak. Just one greeting often reflects its cultural setting.

There are also numerous expressions in Japanese that derive from seasonal happenings and weather. This is mainly due to the sensitivity that Japanese people have had to climate conditions.

You may sense many of these things as you study the language. It is important to learn cultural differences through the language. It is suggested, therefore, that cultural study be made by direct observation of customs or by any available book that may assist you in understanding the people. Better communication will result.

Set apart from cultural emphasis, this book deals strictly with the Japanese language. It is designed to introduce Japanese expressions in the patterns of conversational usage. Primary emphasis is placed, for beginners, on getting acquainted with the language and developing conversational skills by learning important basic structures and patterns. In order not to fall into any monotony, quite a number of useful expressions are introduced, which may have to be learned through mimicry, in addition to drills and exercises. The exercises cover not only one lesson but, on an accumulated basis, previous lessons.

What you must be alert for when you study the language is to avoid getting bored. Language study should be fun. Each lesson has been compiled to give simple patterns so that they may be digested easily enough to apply to conversation. Each lesson is independent with introduction of new structures and useful expressions. Drills cover new structures that must be memorized to the extent that they can immediately be used in a practical way. It is a MUST to work on the drills intensively. Often there are new vocabularies without English meaning. For this reason, it is recommended that you have a dictionary with you all of the time.

At the end of this book are Charts of Adjectives, Noun-Adjectives and Verbs with pattern sentences that may help you study as you advance. It is the author's sincere hope that all the lessons and supplemental charts will be found very understandable and that you will enjoy speaking Japanese soon.

Finally, the author wishes to extend his thanks to Dale P. Crowley, linguist, for his "Conversational Japanese Structure Drill Manual," published in 1964, as it has been of great help in writing this book. He also thanks his wife, Yoko, who has given so many suggestions and input from her experience in teaching at Hawaii Community College at the University of Hawaii at Hilo. Also, he thanks Mark Waters for drawing the illustrations and Mrs. Frances Reed for helping with the proof reading. All their help has made this book better.

May God help your study.

Yoshiyuki Kawata
September, 1976

Doko e ikimasu ka.

Kanada wa samui desu ka.

Hawai wa atatakai desu.

Nihon wa ima samui deshoo.

LESSON ONE

DOKO E IKIMASU KA

Yamada: Ohayoo gozaimasu, Sumisu san.
Sumisu: Ohayoo gozaimasu, Yamada san.
Yamada: Doko e ikimasu ka.
Sumisu: San Furanshisuko e ikimasu.
Yamada: San Furanshisuko wa ima samui desu ka.
Sumisu: Hai, tabun samui deshoo.
Yamada: Sore dewa, ki o tsukete, itte irasshai.
Sumisu: Sayoonara.

MEANING

WHERE ARE YOU GOING?

Yamada: Good morning, Mr. Smith.
Smith: Good morning, Mr. Yamada.
Yamada: Where are you going?
Smith: I am going to San Francisco.
Yamada: Is it cold in San Francisco now?
Smith: Yes, it must probably be cold.
Yamada: Well then, take care and good-bye.
Smith: Good-bye.

STRUCTURES

1.	Doko e ikimasu ka	Interrogative word, Doko + relator particle, e + verb, ikimasu + ending particle for question, ka
2.	San Furanshisuko e ikimasu	Proper noun, San Furanshisuko + realator particle, e + verb, ikimasu
3.	San Furanshisuko wa ima samui desu ka	Nominative, San Furanshisuko + relator particle, wa + time slot, ima + adjective, samui + Copula, desu + ka
4.	Tabun samui deshoo	Adverb, tabun + adjective, samui + Copula, deshoo

USEFUL EXPRESSIONS

Ohayoo gozaimasu — "Good morning." When meeting somebody in the morning time, usually this greeting is exchanged, but since the literal meaning of "Ohayoo" is "early," the greeting changes from late morning, say, about 11 o'clock to "Kon'nich wa" when the sun is way up.

Ki o tsukete — "Be careful" or "Take care." This expression is often used by itself or with an ending particle "ne" like "Ki o tsukete ne" meaning "Take care,

	okay?" In the dialog, however, it is described as meaning "taking care of yourself," which is a participial construction in English and must be completed by another statement to follow. (Note: This pattern will be learned at a little advanced level.)
Itte irasshai	This literally means "Go and come back." It is a typical expression used by a person staying back at home or office, etc. to somebody in-group who is leaving. For instance, a house wife customarily uses this expression to her husband or child who is leaving, or an office girl to her boss, etc.
Itte mairimasu	"I am going." Interchangeably used with "Itte irasshai," when leaving home, office, etc.

GRAMMER GENERALIZATIONS

Doko e ikimasu ka.

"Doko" is an interrogative word which is equivalent to "where" in English. Whereas English composes sentence structures with prepositions such as to, in, on, at, etc., Japanese take postpositional structures. This is one of the characteristics of the Japanese language.

Now, the Japanese postpositional "e" is a relator particle (also known as relational) for goal movement and always used after some place to go. Examples:

| Doko e | Where (Lit. to where) |
| Honoruru e | to Honoruru |

"ikimasu" is a verbal form meaning "go." The verbal form "-masu" is polite affirmative and non-past tense.

"ikimasu ka" - the last ending particle is for a question. To make a question in Japanese is rather simple, because all you have to do is to put "ka" at the end of a sentence. Compare the following two sentences:

| Tookyoo e ikimasu. | I am going to Tokyo. |
| Tookyoo e ikimasu ka. | Are you going to Tokyo? |

San Furanshisuko e ikimasu.

In the presentation dialog Mr. Smith did not specifically mention "watakushi" that means "I." Often Japanese people do not put a subject to identify as far as it is mutually understood in the course of conversation.

| (Anata wa) Doko e ikimasu ka. | Naturally asking the second person, "you." |

LET'S SPEAK JAPANESE

(Watakushi wa) San Furanshisuko e ikimasu.	Naturally the first person, "I," answering the question.

"ikimasu" is a motion verb. There are other motion verbs as follows.

Kaerimasu	return
kimasu	come

These verbs can be used in the same way as follows.

Doko e kaerimasu ka	Where are you returning?
Tookyoo e kaerimasu.	I am returning to Tokyo.
Doko e kimasu ka.	Where are you (or he or she) coming?
Gakkoo e kimasu.	I am coming to school.

San Furanshisuko wa ima samui desu ka.

When picking up something as a topic, it is always followed by relator particle "wa" immediately. Be sure that you pronounce it right after the nominative.

San Furanshisuko wa

Don't separate it or pause after the topic when pronouncing.

San Furanshisuko . . . wa

"Samui" is an adjective. "Samui desu" is predicate adjective meaning "It is cold." "desu" is equational verb, better known as Copula. Note that "desu" is polite affirmative and present tense.

Hai, tabun samui deshoo.

With the adverb, "tabun," this "deshoo" pattern is frequently used when you guess or assume. The original form of "deshoo" is "desu," the Copula.

cf.	Samui desu.	It is cold.
	Samui deshoo.	I guess it is cold. (It must be cold.)

If you wish to simply answer without any guess, you can say as follows.

San Furanshisuko wa ima samui desu ka.
— Hai, samui desu.

SHORT DIALOGS—MEMORIZE

Dialog 1:

A: Buraun san, ohayoo gozaimasu.
B: Ohayoo gozaimasu, Abe san.
A: Doko e ikimasu ka.
B: Honoruru e ikimasu.

Dialog 2:

A: Honoruru wa ima atatakai desu ka.
B: Hai, tabun atatakai deshoo.
A: Sore dewa, ki o tsukete, itte irasshai.
B: Itte mairimasu.

DRILLS - Questions & Answers

1. Doko e ikimasu ka.   Tookyoo e ikimasu.
2. Doko e ikimasu ka.   Hokkaidoo e ikimasu.
3. Doko e kaerimasu ka.   Nyuuyooku e kaerimasu.
4. Doko e kaerimasu ka.   Shikago e kaerimasu.
5. Doko e kimasu ka.   Oosaka e kimasu.
6. Doko e kimasu ka.   Hawai e kimasu.

Practice more by using the following words.
Furansu (France), Igirisu (England), Nihon (Japan),
Itaria (Italy), Porutogaru (Portugal), Supein (Spain)

DRILLS - Questions & Answers

1. Arasuka wa ima samui desu ka.   Hai, tabun samui deshoo.
2. San Furanshisuko wa ima suzushii   Hai, tabun suzushii
   desu ka.   deshoo.
3. Indo wa ima atsui desu ka.   Hai, tabun atsui deshoo.
4. Nihon wa ima atatakai desu ka.   Hai, tabun atatakai deshoo.

Use the following words and make up questions. Ask
and answer one another.

Rondon (London), Pari (Paris), Washinton (Washington)
Rooma (Rome), Mosukuwa (Moscow), Pekin (Peking)

EXERCISES

1. How do you say the following expressions in Japanese?
   A. Good morning.
   B. Good morning, Mr. Yamada.
   C. Where are you going?
   D. I am going to Tokyo.
   E. Is it cold in Tokyo now?

F. I guess it is probably cold.

2. Answer the following questions according to the given English words.

   A. Doko e ikimasu ka.   (Mexico)
   B. Doko e ikimasu ka.   (Honolulu)
   C. Doko e ikimasu ka.   (Boston)
   D. Doko e ikimasu ka.   (Hong Kong)

3. Make a short dialog according to the following situation.

   Miss Tanaka meets Mr. Johnson in the morning. They greet each other. Miss Tanaka asks Mr. Johnson where he is going. He answers that he is going to New York. Then she asks if it is cold in NewYork now. He answers that it probably is.

LESSON TWO

DOKO DE HON O KAIMASU KA

Joonzu:	Doko de hon o kaimasu ka.
Tanaka:	Depaato de kaimasu.
Joonzu:	Sono depaato wa tooi desu ka.
Tanaka:	Hai, chotto tooi desu ga, totemo ookii desu yo.
Joonzu:	Soko de hoka ni nani o kaimasu ka.
Tanaka:	Soo desu nee . . . Hoka ni wa nani mo kaimasen.

MEANING
WHERE ARE YOU GOING TO BUY A BOOK?

Jones:	Where are you going to buy a book?
Tanaka:	I'll buy it at a department store.
Jones:	Is the department store far?
Tanaka:	Yes, it's a little far, but it's very large to be sure.
Jones:	What else are you going to buy there?
Tanaka:	Let me see . . . I won't buy anything else.

STRUCTURES

1. Doko de hon o kaimasu ka — Interrogative word, Doko + object, hon + relator particle, o + verb, kaimasu + ending particle, ka.

2. Depaato de kaimasu — Place noun, depaato + relator particle, de + verb, kaimasu

3. Sono depaato wa tooi desu ka — Determiner Sono + noun + relator particle, wa + adjective, tooi + desu ka

4. Chotto tooi desu ga — Adverb, chotto + adjective, tooi + desu + conjunction, ga

5. Nani o kaimasu ka — Interrogative word, nani + o + verb, kaimasu + ka

6. Nani mo kaimasen — Pronoun, nani + relator particle, no + verbal negative form, kaimasen

USEFUL EXPRESSION

Nani mo kaimasen — "I don't buy anything" or I won't buy anything." "Nani mo" means anything and it is always used in the negative form of verb. Here are similar expressions in the same structure.

Nani mo tabemasen.   I don't eat anything.
Nani mo nomimasen.   I don't drink anything.

GRAMMAR GENERALIZATIONS

Doko de hon o kaimasu ka.

Here is a new relator particle "de" used after the interrogative word "doko." It functions to indicate a location, but it has to be followed always by a certain action that would take place there. In other words, when a certain location is indicated with this relator particle, a certain action verb usually follows.

Another new relator particle "o" indicates an object. It is used with transtive verbs that need an object. Now, take a look at the sentence, "hon o kaimasu ka." "kaimasu" is a transitive verb working with the object "hon." "ka" is an ending particle for a question as explained before, so this whole meaning goes like this with "doko de" inclusive.

"Where are you going to buy a book?"

Listed below are a few action and transitive verbs.

(Gohan o) tabemasu.	I eat meal.
(Koohii o) nomimasu.	I drink coffee.
(Eiga o) mimasu.	I watch a movie.
(Eigo o) oshiemasu.	I teach English.
(Hon o) yomimasu.	I read a book.
(Tegami o) kakimasu.	I write a letter.
(Rajio o) kikimasu.	I listen to the radio.

Sono depaato wa tooi desu ka.

In this sentence "sono depaato" is a topic, thereby bringing the relator particle "wa" right after. "Tooi" is an adjective meaning "far." "Tooi desu" means "It's far," so naturally with the question particle "ka," it gives a meaning "Is it far?" Whenever you mention something or somebody specifically as a topic, it must immediately be followed by the relator particle "wa," without any pause.

"Sono" is a determiner of which English equivalent is "that." It must be used as a determiner to modify something or somebody. Therefore, it cannot be used by itself as either topic or subject or even as an object. The following is its proper way of usage.

kono gakkoo	this school
sono jimusho	that office
ano kyookai	that church over there
kono hito (or kata)	this person
sono sensei	that teacher
ano gakusei	that student over there

LET'S SPEAK JAPANESE

Note: You can consider this function as possessive form of this, that and that . . . over there in English. There are other forms of these words that will be learned on Lesson 4.

Hai

This is just like English "yes." Whenever you agree with a speaker, you can say "hai," no matter what the question may be. You can even answer with "hai" to negative content of a question if you agree with the speaker. (This is different from English.)

"Hai" is practically same as "Ee" which is often used in conversation.

Chotto tooi desu ga, totemo ookii desu yo.

"Chotto" and "totemo" are adverbs meaning "a little" and "very" respectively. The most important part in this sentence is "ga" which is a conjunction equivalent to "but" in English. Whereas you state "but" to start with a new statement in English after its preceeding statement is completed, "ga" immediately follows the preceeding statement in Japanese. Note the difference:

| It is a little far, but it is very large. | English |
| Chotto tooi desu ga, totemo ookii desu yo. | Japanese |

"Yo" is an ending particle used to emphasize the fact of a statement. Therefore, it can be translated as "for sure," "to be sure," "you know," "you see" or "I am telling you."

| Amerika wa ookii desu yo. | America is big for sure. |
| Sono biichi wa abunai desu yo. | That beach is dangerous to be sure. |

Soko de

This means "there." To indicate the location "soko," "de" has to accompany in this case. Incidentally, note the followings:

| koko de | here |
| asoko de | over there |

Hoka ni

As an idiomatic adverb, it is suggested to memorize this word. It means "except it," "besides" or "in addition."

Nani o kaimasu ka.

"Nani" is an interrogative word meaning "what." This whole sentence is a question with the ending particle ka and the interrogative word "nani" functions as an object of the verb "kaimasu."

The following is a vocabulary list of verbs, adjectives and nouns that can be used for practice in the patterns you have learned on this lesson.

Verbs

kaimasu	buy	yomimasu	read
urimasu	sell	kakimasu	write
tabemasu	eat	mimasu	see, watch
nomimasu	drink	torimasu	take
kikimasu	hear, listen to	oshiemasu	teach

Adjectives

tooi	far	chiisai	small
chikai	close	oishii	delicious
takai	high, expensive	mazui	distasteful
yasui	cheap	ii (yoi)	good
ookii	big	warui	bad
hayai	fast, early	omoshiroi	interesting, fun
osoi	slow, late	tsumaranai	uninteresting

Nouns

Places

gakkoo	school	jinja	shrine
daigaku	university	toshokan	library
kaisha	company	shokudoo	restaurant
jimusho	office	depaato	department store
ginkoo	bank	shashinya	camera shop
byooin	hospital	honya	book store
eigakan	movie theater	hanaya	florist
tokoya (rihatsuten)	barber shop	sakanaya	fish market
kyookai	church	nikuya	meat shop
o-tera	temple (Buddhism)	bunbooguten	stationery shop

Items

hon	book	raisu karei	curry rice
zasshi	magazine	gohan	meal
shinbun	newspaper	ocha	tea
jidoosha	car	koohii	coffee
rajio	radio	koocha	black tea
terebi	television	tegami	letter
isu	chair	shashin	photograph
tsukue	desk	hana	flower
enpitsu	pencil	sakana	fish
pen	pen	niku	meat

All the adjectives end with "i" in combination with the following vowels.

LET'S SPEAK JAPANESE

       ai - like chikai   ui - like mazui
       ii - like oishii   oi - like tooi

SHORT DIALOGS - MEMORIZE

Dialog 1:

A: Doko de zasshi o kaimasu ka.
B: Honya de kaimasu.
A: Sono honya wa yasui desu ka.
B: Hai, Chotto yasui desu ga, totemo tooi desu.

Dialog 2:

A: Doko de kamera o kaimasu ka.
B: Shashinya de kaimasu.
A: Sono shashinya wa yasui desu ka.
B: Hai, chotto yasui desu ga, totemo tooi desu.

DRILLS - Questions & Answers

A:
1. Doko de pen o kaimasu ka.   Bunbooguten de kaimasu.
2. Doko de shinbun o yomimasu ka.   Uchi de yomimasu.
3. Doko de gohan o tabemasu ka.   Shokudoo de tabemasu.
4. Doko de ongaku o kikimasu ka.   Gakkoo de kikimasu.
5. Doko de shashin o torimasu ka.   Daigaku de torimasu.
6. Doko de tegami o kakimasu ka.   Kaisha de kakimasu.
7. Doko de koohii o nomimasu ka.   Jimusho de nomimasu.
8. Doko de eiga o mimasu ka.   Nihon Gekijoo de mimasu.

B:
1. Sono ginkoo wa tooi desu ka.   Hai, tooi desu.
2. Sono shashinya wa chikai desu ka.   Hai, chikai desu.
3. Sono nikuya wa ookii desu ka.   Hai, ookii desu.
4. Sono shinbun wa takai desu ka.   Hai, takai desu.

C:
1. Sono hanaya wa chikai desu ka.   Hai, chikai desu ga, totemo chiisai desu.
2. Sono zasshi wa yasui desu ka.   Hai, yasui desu ga, totemo omoshiroi desu.
3. Sono byooin wa tooi desu ka.   Hai, tooi desu ga, totemo ii desu.
4. Sono sakana wa oishii desu ka.   Hai, oishii desu ga, totemo takai desu.

D:
1. Soko de hoka ni nani o kaimasu ka   Soo desu nee . . . Hoka ni nani mo kaimasen.
2. Soko de hoka ni nani o tabemasu ka. Soo desu nee . . . Hoka ni nani mo tabemasen.
3. Soko de hoka ni nani o yomimasu ka. Soo desu nee . . . Hoka ni nani mo yomimasen.
4. Soko de hoka ni nani o kakimasu ka. Soo desu nee . . . Hoka ni

nani mo kakimasen.

DRILLS - Simple Questions & Answers

A: Verbs

1. Doko de tabemasu ka   Koko de tabemasu.
                                             Soko de tabemasu.
                                             Asoko de tabemasu.

2. Doko de kaimasu ka.   Koko de kaimasu.
                                             Soko de kaimasu.
                                             Asoko de kaimasu.

3. Doko de yomimasu ka.   Koko de yomimasu.
                                             Soko de yomimasu.
                                             Asoko de yomimasu.

4. Doko de urimasu ka.   Koko de urimasu.
                                             Soko de urimasu.
                                             Asoko de urimasu.

B: Adjectives

1. Kaisha wa chikai desu ka.   Hai, chikai desu.
2. Jimusho wa ookii desu ka.   Hai, ookii desu.
3. Terebi wa omoshiroi desu ka.   Hai, omoshiroi desu.
4. Eiga wa tsumaranai desu ka.   Hai, tsumaranai desu.
5. Kyookai wa chiisai desu ka.   Hai, chiisai desu.
6. Sono niku wa mazui desu ka.   Hai, mazui desu.
7. Kono isu wa yasui desu ka.   Hai, yasui desu.
8. Ano jidoosha wa takai desu ka.   Hai, takai desu.
9. Sono gakkoo wa tooi desu ka.   Hai, tooi desu.
10. Kono honya wa ii desu ka.   Hai, ii desu.

EXERCISES

1. How do you say the following expressions in Japanese?

    1. Where are you going to buy a book?   I'll buy it at a department store.
    2. Where are you going to watch TV?   I'll watch TV at home.
    3. Where are you going to eat your meal?   I'll eat over there.
    4. Where are you going to write a letter?   I'll write it in the library.
    5. Is the school far?   Yes, it is.
    6. Is the bank small?   Yes, it is small, but it is very close.
    7. Is the pencil cheap?   Yes, it is.
    8. What else are you going to buy?   I won't buy anything else.

LET'S SPEAK JAPANESE

2. Fill in with proper expressions on the underlines.

   S: _____ , Tanaka san. _____
       Good morning   Where are you going?
   T: _____
       I am going to Tokyo.
   S: _____
       What are you going to buy in Tokyo?
   T: _____
       I am going to buy a TV.

3. Fill in each blank with a proper relator particle.

   1. Doko (   ) ikimasu ka.
   2. Soko (   ) hon (   ) kaimasu.
   3. Uchi (   ) ima kaerimasu.
   4. Uchi (   ) terebi (   ) mimasu.
   5. Nihon (   ) ima samui desu ka.
   6. Toshokan (   ) hon (   ) yomimasu.
   7. Tanaka san wa koko (   ) kimasu.

4. Make a short dialog based on the following situation.

   Mr. Saito meets Miss Davis in the morning. They greet each other. Mr. Saito asks Miss Davis where she is going to read a book. She says she is going to read it in the library. Now, he asks if the library is far. She answers that it is a little far but it is very large. Mr. Saito further asks if she is going to read anything else there. She thinks for a moment and answers that she won't read anything else.

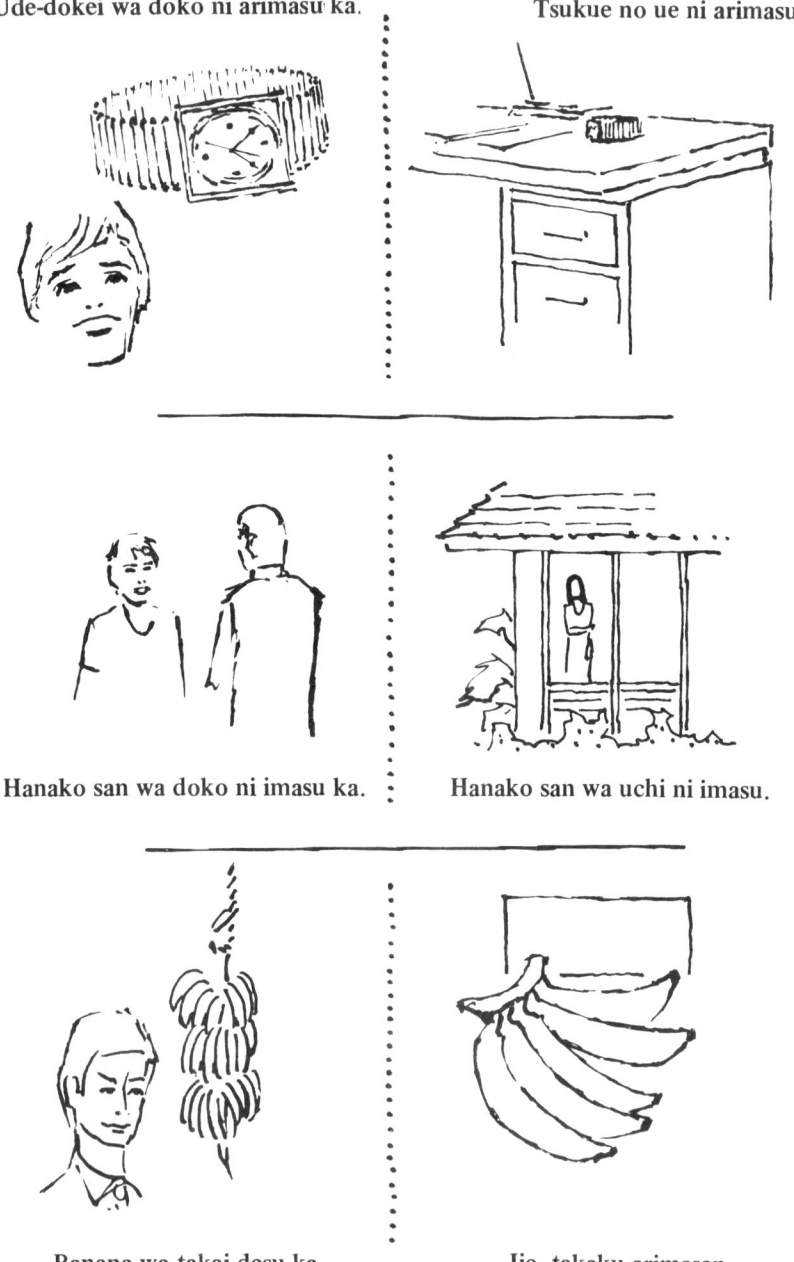

Ude-dokei wa doko ni arimasu ka.   Tsukue no ue ni arimasu.

Hanako san wa doko ni imasu ka.   Hanako san wa uchi ni imasu.

Banana wa takai desu ka.   Iie, takaku arimasen.

LESSON THREE

DAIGAKU WA DOKO NI ARIMASU KA
SENSEI WA DOKO NI IMASU KA

— MICHI DE —

Buraun:	Daigaku wa doko ni arimasu ka.
Kimura:	Katorikku kyookai no soba ni arimasu.
Buraun:	Koko kara tooi desu ka.
Kimura:	Iie, amari tooku arimasen yo. Ano ookii tatemono desu.
Buraun:	Soo desu ka. Doomo arigatoo gozaimasu.

— Koonai De —

Buraun:	Chotto shitsurei desu ga, Yamada sensei wa doko ni imasu ka.
Gakusei:	Sensei wa jimusho ni imasu yo.
Buraun:	Doomo arigatoo gozaimasu.
Gakusei:	Doo itashimashite.

MEANING
— On the Street —

Brown:	Where is the university?
Kimura:	It is by the Catholic Church.
Brown:	Is it far from here?
Kimura:	No, it is not so far to be sure. It is that big building over there.
Brown:	Is that so? Thank you very much.

— On the Campus —

Brown:	Excuse me, but where is Professor Yamada?
Student:	He is in the office.
Brown:	Thank you very much.
Student:	Don't memtion it.

STRUCTURES

1. Daigaku wa doko ni arimasu ka — Nominative + wa + interrogative word doko + relator particle ni + + existence verb arimasu + ka

2. Amari tooku arimasen yo — Adverb amari + negative adjective, tooku arimasen + ending particle yo

3. Ano ookii tatemono desu — Determiner ano + adjective ookii + noun tatemono + Copula desu

4. Sensei wa jimusho ni imasu — Nominative + wa + place noun

jimusho + relator particle ni + existence verb imasu.

USEFUL EXPRESSIONS

Doomo arigatoo gozaimasu
"Thank you very much." This can often be shortened as follows.

"Doomo arigatoo."
"Doomo."   less polite
"Arigatoo."

Chotto shitsurei desu ga,
This literally means "It is a little impolite, but . . . " Usually this is translated as "Excuse me, but..." Chotto means "a little" or "for a moment." Whenever you ask somebody especially a stranger, about something, you can use this expression to get started.

Doo itashimashite
"You are welcome.", "Don't mention it." or "Not at all." (This sounds like "Don't touch my mustache" but it isn't.)

GRAMMAR GENERALIZATIONS

Daigaku wa doko ni arimasu ka.

In the previous lesson you learned "doko de" that means where and that when the relator particle "de" is used, it is followed usually by an action verb to indicate that something would happen there.

Now, "doko ni" is another combination of "doko" and relator particle "ni" that is also for a location. In this case, however, it must be followed by an existence verb indicating that something or somebody exists in the location. Whenever you mention a place with "ni," always be sure that a certain thing (not event or happening) or somebody has to be described for existence.

The verb "arimasu" is an existence verb which can be used for inanimate things. In the presentation dialog Mr. Brown picked up "daigaku" to ask where it is. "Daigaku" is inanimate. Therefore, it is followed by the verb "arimasu."

cf. Doko de gohan o tabemasu ka.   – right
     Doko ni gohan o tabemasu ka.   – wrong

     Daigaku wa doko ni arimasu ka. – right
     Daigaku wa doko de arimasu ka. – wrong

("de arimasu" is not proper in this case. "De arimasu" is a speech form of desu, which was also often used in the military during the war time. "Desu" functions exactly for the same meaning as "ni arimasu" and so "de arimasu" is seemingly alright, but it is not appropriate to use it conversationally because it sounds like a speech or military expression.)

If there is a certain event or happening that can be described in one word or phrase, the relator particle for that location should be "de" with the verb "arimasu." This is because the event is a sort of action. Example:

    Daigaku de eiga ga arimasu.   There will be a movie in the university.

Katorikku kyookai no soba ni

This means "by the Catholic Church." As one of the most frequently used idiomatic phrases it is suggested to memorize and use it often. It is a combination of a certain place and idiomatic relator particle "no soba ni." Outlined below are some similar phrases.

gakkoo no chikaku ni	near school
toshokan no yoko ni	on the side of the library
yama no ue ni	on the mountain
tsukue no shita ni	under the desk
uchi no naka ni	inside the house
gareeji no mae ni	in front of the garage
daigaku no ushiro ni	in the back of the university

(NOTE: The relator particle part, "ni," is flexible, depending on what is to come after. If a certain action takes place, then it has to be changed to "de" for the location.)

Koko kara tooi desu ka.

"Kara" is a relator particle equivalent to "from" in English. It can be used simply as follows.

Tookyoo kara	from Tokyo
Nihon Kara	from Japan
Kaisha kara	from the company
kanojo kara	from her (or girlfriend)
chichi kara	from my father
haha kara	from my mother
koko kara	from here
soko kara	from there
asoko kara	from over there

Iie, amari tooku arimasen yo.

"Iie" is just like English "no." If you disagree with the speaker, you can answer with "iie," no matter what contents the question may have - whether it is affirmative or negative. "Amari tooku arimasen" means "It's not too far." The most important part is the negative form of adjective which conjugates from affirmative form as follows.

>tooi desu —— tooku arimasen

All the adjectives carry "i" at the end, which is very clue for conjugation. To change from the affirmative form to the negative form the final -i must be completely dropped off so that it may be replaced by -ku and followed by "arimasen" instead of "desu."

NOTE: Practically the final -i must be cut off always to form past tense, negative past tense, conditional form, etc. on adjectives.

Ano ookii tatemono desu.

Adjectives have a function like English to modify nouns in the plain form. It may be one of the easiest patterns for a Japanese learning student to master because it is formed in the same way as English. "Ano ookii tatemono" is "that big building over there." To get used to the form, note the following.

kono takai kudamono	This expensive fruit.
Sono omoshiroi hon	That interesting book.
Ano chiisai ike	That small pond over there.

Yamada sensei wa doko ni imasu ka.

"Imasu" is an existence verb which is used for animate being. You can compare this verb with another verb you have just learned for inanimate things. Although the meaning of both verbs is exactly same, their usage is different, depending on what subject or topic to come along.

Animate:	Umi ni sakana ga imasu.	There are fish in the sea.
Inanimate:	Mise ni sakana ga arimasu.	There are fish in the store.

While the fish in the sea are alive, the fish in the store are already dead ones in this case. Therefore, you can consider the fish in the store as an inanimate object.

The following are some expressions with the verb, "imasu."

Sensei wa jimusho ni imasu.	The teacher is in the office.
Daitooryoo wa Hakuakan ni imasu.	The President is in the White House.
Chiji wa ima Nyuuyooku ni imasu.	The Governor is now in New York.

LET'S SPEAK JAPANESE

Inu wa niwa ni imasu.	The dog is in the yard.
Ushi wa bokujoo ni imasu.	The cattle are in the pasture.
Hato wa yane ni imasu.	The pigeon is on the roof.

SHORT DIALOGS - MEMORIAZE

Dialog 1:

A: Hikoojoo wa doko ni arimasu ka.
B: Kooen no chikaku ni arimasu.
A: Koko kara tooi desu ka.
B: Iie, amari tooku arimasen yo.
   Ano nagai tatemono desu.
A: Soo desu ka. Doomo arigatoo gozaimasu.

Dialog 2:

A: Chotto shitsurei desu ga, Tanaka san wa doko ni imasu ka.
B: Tanaka san wa koojoo ni imasu yo.
A: Doomo arigatoo gozaimasu.
B: Doo itashimashite.

The following is a vocabulary list that may be referred to for your practice.

hoteru	hotel	shooken gaisha	security company
maaketto	market	fudoosan gaisha	real estate company
keisatsusho	police station	soogisho	funeral hall
shooboosho	fire station	gasorin sutando	gas station
saibansho	court	eki	station
yuubinkyoku	post office	hikoojoo	airport
gasu gaisha	gas company	kooen	park
denki gaisha	electric company	koojoo or kooba	factory
denwakyoku	telephone company	yakkyoku	pharmacy
kin'yuu gaisha	financial company	heya	room

DRILLS - Questions & Answers

A: 1. Hoteru wa doko ni arimasu ka.   Kooen no soba ni arimasu.
   2. Yuubinkyoku wa doko ni arimasu ka.   Daigaku no soba ni arimasu.
   3. Kaisha wa doko ni arimasu ka.   Eki no soba ni arimasu.
   4. Gasorin sutando wa doko ni arimasu ka. Yakkyoku no soba ni arimasu.

B: 1. Saibansho wa doko ni arimasu ka.   Gakkoo no chikaku ni arimasu.
   2. Keisatsusho wa doko ni arimasu ka.   Hikoojoo no chikaku ni arimasu.
   3. Maaketto wa doko ni arimasu   Hoteru no chikaku ni arimasu.

ka.
4. Fudoosan gaisha wa doko ni arimasu ka.   Eki no chikaku ni arimasu.

C: 1. Enpitsu wa doko ni arimasu ka.   Tsukue no ue ni arimasu.
    2. Rajio wa doko ni arimasu ka.   Heya no naka ni arimasu.
    3. Shinbun wa doko ni arimasu ka.   Terebi no yoko ni arimasu.
    4. Tegami wa doko ni arimasu ka.   Shorui no shita ni arimasu.

DRILLS - In reference to the following pictures, complete each sentence accordingly.

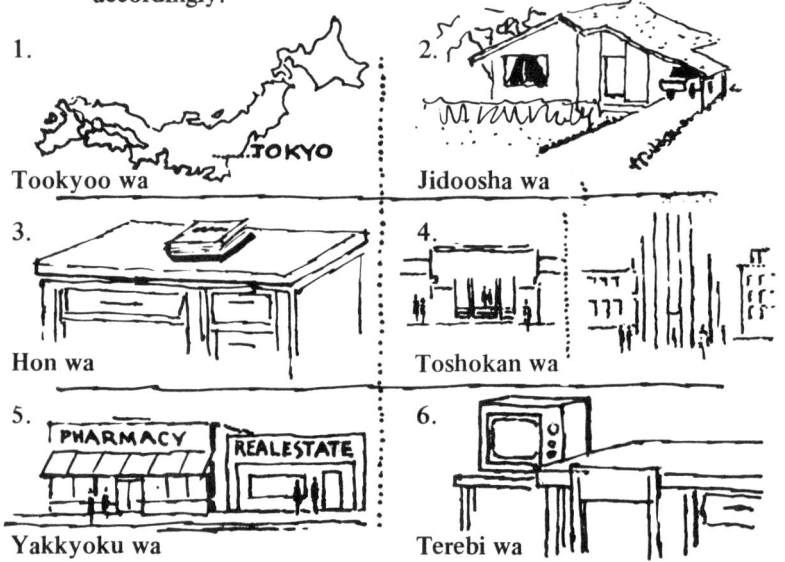

1. Tookyoo wa
2. Jidoosha wa
3. Hon wa
4. Toshokan wa
5. Yakkyoku wa
6. Terebi wa

DRILLS - Questions & Answers

A: 1. Sensei wa doko ni imasu ka.   Jimusho ni imasu.
    2. Saitoo san wa doko ni imasu ka.   Gakkoo ni imasu.
    3. Gakusei wa doko ni imasu ka.   Toshokan ni imasu.
    4. Chichi wa doko ni imasu ka.   Kaisha ni imasu.

B: 1. Inu wa doko ni imasu ka.   Niwa ni imasu.
    2. Neko wa doko ni imasu ka.   Uchi ni imasu.
    3. Ushi wa doko ni imasu ka.   Bokujoo ni imasu.
    4. Uma wa doko ni imasu ka.   Asoko ni imasu.

LET'S SPEAK JAPANESE

DRILLS - Questions & Answers (Negative Form of Adjectives)

A: 1. Koko kara tooi desu ka.   Iie, amari tooku arimasen.
   2. Koko kara chikai desu ka.   Iie, amari chikaku arimasen.
   3. Tookyoo kara tooi desu ka.   Iie, amari tooku arimasen.
   4. Oosaka kara chikai desu ka. Iie, amari chikaku arimasen.

B: 1. Kono ringo wa oishii desu ka.   Iie, oishiku arimasen.
   2. Sono jimusho wa ookii desu ka. Iie, ookiku arimasen.
   3. Ano daigaku wa chiisai desu ka. Iie, chiisaku arimasen.
   4. Sono banana wa takai desu ka.   Iie, takaku arimasen.

C: Make up a few questions by using adjectives and answer accordingly in the negative form.

EXERCISES:

1. How do you say the following expressions in Japanese?

    1. Thank you very much.
    2. You are welcome.
    3. The university is near the station.
    4. Miss Yamamoto is in the office.
    5. Excuse me, but where is the post office?

2. Put "de" or "ni" in a blank.

    1. Shokudoo (   ) gohan o tabemasu.
    2. Gakkoo wa eki no soba (   ) arimasu.
    3. Chichi wa kaisha (   ) imasu.
    4. Toshokan (   ) hon o yomimasu.
    5. Toshokan wa daigaku (   ) arimasu.

3. Make a situational conversation.

    Hanako meets Tom on the street and asks him where Mr. Smith is. Tom answers that he is in the company. Hanako further asks Tom where the company is. Then, pointing to the company, Tom tells that it is over there. Hanako thanks Tom and leaves.

Ashita Nihon kara katoo san ga kimasu ne.

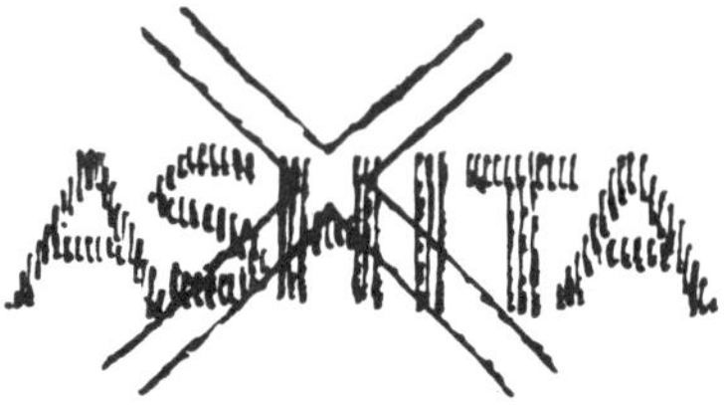

Iie, mada kimasen yo.

Itsu kimasu ka.

Tabun raishuu deshoo.

Ashita nani o shimasu ka.

Ashita wa uchi de benkyoo shimasu.

LET'S SPEAK JAPANESE

LESSON FOUR

MADA KIMASEN YO

Masako: Raishuu Kanada kara Saitoo san ga kimasu ne.
Toshio: Iie, mada kimasen yo.
Masako: Itsu kimasu ka.
Toshio: Tabun raigetsu deshoo. Tokorode, ashita nani o shimasu ka.
Masako: Ashita wa uchi de benkyoo shimasu.
Toshio: Soo desu ka. Kanshin desu nee.

MEANING

HE IS NOT COMING YET

Masako: Mr. Saito is coming from Canada next week, isn't he?
Toshio: No, he is not coming yet.
Masako: When is he coming?
Toshio: I guess (he'll be back) probably next month. By the way, what are you going to do tomorrow?
Masako: I will study at home tomorrow.
Toshio: Is that right! You are admirable.

STRUCTURES

1. Raishuu Kanada kara saitoo san ga kimasu ne — Time slot raishuu + place noun Kanada + relator particle kara + nominative (a person Saitoo san) + relator particle ga + irregular verb kimasu + ending particle ne

2. Mada kimasen yo — Time slot (adverb) mada + verbal negative form (of kimasu) + yo

3. Itsu kimasu ka — Interrogative word Itsu + irregular verb kimasu + ka

4. Tabun raigetsu deshoo — Adverb tabun + time noun raigetsu + oo form of Copula

5. Ashita nani o shimasu ka — Time slot ashita + interrogative word nani + o + irregular verb shimasu + ka

USEFUL EXPRESSIONS

Nani o shimasu ka — "What are you going to do? See Grammar Generalizations.

Kanshin desu nee — "You are admirable." When you

admire somebody's act, this expression is used.

GRAMMAR GENERALIZATIONS

Raishuu Kanada kara Saitoo san ga kimasu ne.

"Raishuu" is a time slot meaning "next week." There are words as listed below in relation to this type of time slot.

*	kinoo	yesterday	*	sengetsu	last month
	kyoo	today		kongetsu	this month
	ashita	tomorrow		raigetsu	next month
*	sakuban	last night	*	kyonen	last year
	(kinoo no ban)			kotoshi	this year
	konban	tonight		rainen	next year
	myooban	tomorrow night			
	(ashita no ban)				
*	senshuu	last week			
	konshuu	this week			
	raishuu	next week			

The words with asterisk cannot be used with the verb of -masu or -masen form because they are time slots for past tense.

What is new and important in the above sentence is a relator particle "ga." When it is used, it is more emphatic on the subject than the relator particle "wa" which is for a topic.

There is a difference between these two relator particles, even though they can be seemingly used in the same sentence structure. See the following.

Saitoo san wa kimasu ne.	As for Mr. Saito, he is coming, isn't he?
Saitoo san ga kimasu ne.	Mr. Saito is coming, isn't he? (Not others, but Mr. Saito is coming, isn't he?)

Mr. Saito as a subject is emphasized on the second sentence. In other words, when "ga" is used, attention is more focused on its subject.

Iie, mada kimasen yo.

"No, he is not coming yet for sure." "Mada" is a time slot equivalent to "still" or "not yet."

Mada tabemasen.	I don't eat it yet.
Ano hito wa mada kimasu.	That person is still coming.

LET'S SPEAK JAPANESE

"Kimasen" is the negative form of "kimasu" which is considered as one of the two irregular verbs due to its irregular changes of stem part for conjugation.

Irregular Verb "kimasu"

konai	(Plain negative)
kimasu	(This is the form on this lesson)
kuru	(Plain affirmative)
kureba	(Conditional)
koi	(Command)

"-masen" is the negative form of "-masu."

kaimasu	kaimasen
tabemasu	tabemasen
mimasu	mimasen
yomimasu	yomimasen

Itsu kimasu ka.

"Itsu" is an interrogative word equivalent to "when." It is simple to make a question like this. Since it is interrogative, the ending particle "ka" must be put at the end of the sentence.

Itsu tabemasu ka.	When are you going to eat?
Itsu mimasu ka.	When are you going to watch?
Itsu kaimasu ka.	When are you going to buy it?
Itsu yomimasu ka.	When are you going to read it?
Itsu kaerimasu ka.	When are you going to return?

You can use "itsu" to simply question as follows.

Itsu desu ka.	When is it?
Itsu.	When?

Tabun raigetsu deshoo.

"Tabun" is an adverb meaning "probably," "maybe" or "perhaps." Just like English there is a similar word in Japanese, that can be interchangeably used.

Osoraku

Osoraku raigetsu deshoo.

OO form of Copula desu, i.e. "deshoo" was introduced in Lesson One. Noun and noun-adjective take the same pattern for conjugation of Copula.

Noun: Tabun raigetsu deshoo.   - It must probably be next month.

Noun-Adj: Tabun kirei deshoo.   - It must probably be pretty.

Ashita nani o shimasu ka.

The verb "shimasu" is new here. It is another irregular verb that conjugates as follows, with irregular change of stem part.

Irregular Verb "shimasu"

shinai	(Plain negative)
* shimasu	(This is the form on this lesson)
suru	(Plain affirmative)
sureba	(Conditional)
shiro	(Command)

The verb means "do" in English and it has wide usage in connection with all sorts of activities as well as sports. Therefore, when the question described as "Nani o shimasu ka" has been given, it expects an answer of some kind of doing from a listener. Examples:—

Nani o shimasu ka.	Uchi de gohan o tabemasu. (I am going to eat a meal at home.)
Nani o shimasu ka.	Toshokan de hon o yomimasu. (I am going to read a book at the library.)

Furthermore, so many different meaning of verbs can be produced in combination with doing type of nouns.

benkyoo (o) shimasu	study
ryokoo shimasu	travel
kaimono shimasu	do shopping
ryoori shimasu	cook
kenkyuu shimasu	research
kooshoo shimasu	negotiate
kekkon shimasu	get married
rikon shimasu	divorce
shigoto (o) shimasu	work
gorufu o shimasu	play golf
yakyuu o shimasu	play baseball
futtobooru o shimasu	play football
tenisu o shimasu	play tennis

There are hundreds of words being frequently used with the irregular verb. All the sports are practically combined with this verb to make up the verbs such as "play ping-pong," "play basketball," etc. and even "ski" and "skate" can be described as "suki o shimasu" and "sukeeto o shimasu" respectively.

Ashita wa

This specifically means "tomorrow" as a topic of the conversation. Therefore, when asked what to do tomorrow, Masako picked up tomorrow as a

LET'S SPEAK JAPANESE

topic to talk about what she is going to do on that day.

NOTE: As far as predicate follows at the end, Japanese sentence doesn't sound funny and it is perfectly alright on structure wise. The only difference is that the word or phrase right before the predicate is slightly emphatic.

1. Raishuu Kanada kara Saitoo san ga kimasu ne.
   Time   Adverbial   Subject   Predicate
   Slot   Phrase

2. Kanada kara Saitoo san ga raishuu kimasu ne.

3. Saitoo san ga raishuu Kanada kara kimasu ne.

In other words, all the phrases before predicate are interchangeable.

SHORT DIALOGS - MEMORIZE

Dialog 1:

A: Ashita Honoruru kara Wakita san ga kimasu ne.
B: Iie, mada kimasen yo.
A: Itsu kimasu ka.
B: Tabun raigetsu deshoo.

Dialog 2:

A: Ashita nani o shimasu ka.
B: Ashita wa uchi de shigoto o shimasu.
A: Soo desu ka. Kanshin desu nee.

DRILLS - Questions & Answers

A:
1. Rainen Oosaka kara Tanaka san ga kimasu ne.   Iie, mada kimasen yo.
2. Ashita Tookyoo kara Kishi san ga kimasu ne.   Iie, mada kimasen yo.
3. Raishuu Hokkaidoo kara Hayashi san ga kimasu ne.   Iie, mada kimasen yo.
4. Raigetsu Rondon kara Sandaasu san ga kimasu ne.   Iie, mada kimasen yo.

Make up questions on your own by using this pattern.

B:
1. Ashita nani o shimasu ka.   Kaimono o shimasu.
2. Raishuu nani o shimasu ka.   Repooto o kakimasu.
3. Raigetsu nani o shimasu ka.   Ryokoo shimasu.
4. Rainen nani o shimasu ka.   Benkyoo shimasu.

C:
1. Kyoo nani o benkyoo shimasu ka.   Nihongo o benkyoo shimasu.
2. Ashita nani o mimasu ka.   Eiga o mimasu.
3. Konshuu nani o kaimasu ka.   Jidoosha o kaimasu.
4. Raishuu nani o yomimasu ka.   Shoosetsu o yomimasu.

DRILLS

A: Practice on "Itsu"

1. Itsu kimasu ka.   Rainen kimasu.
2. Itsu tabemasu ka.   Ima tabemasu.
3. Itsu yomimasu ka.   Ashita yomimasu.
4. Itsu kaerimasu ka.   Konban kaerimasu.
5. Itsu ikimasu ka.   Raishuu ikimasu.
6. Itsu kaimasu ka.   Kyoo kaimasu.
7. Itsu shimasu ka.   Kongetsu shimasu.
8. Itsu nomimasu ka.   Ima nomimasu.
9. Itsu benkyoo shimasu ka.   Myooban benkyoo shimasu.
10. Itsu kakimasu ka.   Konban kakimasu.

B: Practice on "Tabun"

1. Tabun ashita deshoo.
2. Tabun raishuu deshoo.
3. Tabun raigetsu deshoo.
4. Tabun rainen deshoo.

C: Practice on "Tokorode"

1. Tokorode, ashita nani o shimasu ka.   Ashita wa uchi de hon o yomimasu.
2. Tokorode, ashita nani o mimasu ka.   Ashita wa yakyuu o mimasu.
3. Tokorode, kyoo doko e ikimasu ka.   Kyoo wa machi e ikimasu.
4. Tokorode, kyoo doko de kaimasu ka.   Kyoo wa depaato de kaimasu.

D: Practice on "Ashita wa"

1. Ashita wa machi de kaimono o shimasu.
2. Ashita wa toshokau de hon o yomimasu.
3. Ashita wa jimusho de tegami o kakimasu.
4. Ashita wa kaisha de shigoto o shimasu.

LET'S SPEAK JAPANESE

EXERCISES

1. How do you say the following expressions in Japanese?

    1. What are you going to do?
    2. What are you going to do tomorrow?
    3. I am going to study at home tomorrow.
    4. You are admirable.

2. Answer the following questions accordingly.

    1. Raishuu San Furanshisuko kara Kaneko san ga kimasu ne.
    2. Sensei wa itsu kimasu ka.
    3. Itsu Yamamoto san ga kimasu ka.
    4. Ashita doko e ikimasu ka.
    5. Raishuu nani o shimasu ka.
    6. Gakkoo wa koko kara tooi desu ka.
    7. Tokorode, sensei wa jimusho ni imasu ka.
    8. Nihon wa ima samui desu ka.
    9. Ashita nani o kaimasu ka.
    10. Rainen doko e ikimasu ka.

3. Write one sentence each by using the following words.

    1. Rainen
    2. mada
    3. itsu
    4. tabun
    5. tokorode

4. Make a short dialog between two persons about Mr. Smith who is coming back from Paris next week.

Kyoo wa yoi o-tenki desu ne.

Are wa nan desu ka.

Ano rippa na tatemono desu ka.

LESSON FIVE

ARE WA NAN DESU KA

Sugita: Kon'nichi wa, Teiraa san.
(fujin)
Teiraa: Kon'nichi wa, Sugita san no okusan.
Sugita: Kyoo wa yoi o-tenki desu ne.
Teiraa: Ee, hontoo ni yoi o-tenki desu nee. Sugita san, are wa nan desu ka.
Sugita: Ano rippa na tatemono desu ka. Are wa shinbunsha no tatemono desu yo.
Teiraa: Soo desu ka. Zuibun ookii desu nee. Atarashii desu ka.
Sugita: Iie, son'na ni atarashiku arimasen.

MEANING

WHAT IS THAT OVER THERE?

Sugita: Good afternoon, Mr. Tailer.
(Mrs.)
Tailer: Good afternoon, Mrs. Sugita.
Sugita: It's a good weather today, isn't it?
Tailer: Yes, it is a good weather indeed! Mrs. Sugita, what is that over there?
Sugita: Is that fine building over there? That is a building of newspaper company.
Tailer: Is that so! It's extremely big, isn't it! Is that new?
Sugita: No, it's not that new.

STRUCTURES

1. Sugita san no okusan — Proper noun Sugita san + possessive relator particle no + noun
2. Ano rippa na tatemono desu ka. — Determiner ano + noun-adjective rippa na + noun

USEFUL EXPRESSIONS

Son'na ni atarashiku arimasen — "It's not that new." "Son'na ni" is often used as a modifier. It is equivalent to "that much" in English.

GRAMMAR GENERALIZATIONS

Sugita san no okusan

To call somebody's wife they often mention her family name and identify her as her husband's wife. Therefore, "Sugita san no okusan" is literally meaning "Mr. Sugita's wife."

"No" is a relator particle for possessive or belonging just like English "-'s" or the preposition, "of."

Yoi o-tenki desu nee

"Yoi" is the same adjective as "ii." "Yoi" can be used in lieu of "ii" to modify something. "O" of "o-tenki" is a polite prefix of noun. There are certain items to take this prefix. Examples:

sakana	o-sakana
niku	o-niku
mise	o-mise
sara	o-sara
chawan	o-chawan
shooyu	o-shooyu
sake	o-sake
sashimi	o-sashimi
genki	o-genki
joozu	o-joozu

Instead of "o," sometimes "go" is used, depending on the word.

kazoku	go-kazoku (your or somebody's family)
kyoodai	go-kyoodai (your or somebody's brothers or sisters)
byooki	go-byooki (your or somebody's illness)

Ano rippa na tatemono desu ka.

"You mean that fine building over there?" To make sure about what the other party is questioning, she pointed the building and gave this statement in which there is a connotation, "You mean . . . "

The modification form of noun-adjectives always carries "na" as above. In English there is not such part of speech (noun-adjectives) because it is classified under adjectives. Due to the difference of conjugations as well as the modification form of this unique part of speech, it has to be separated from adjectives in Japanese. It functions like an adjective alright, as far as its descriptive pattern in the present tense is concerned, but when it comes to conjugations, it takes altogether different forms from adjectives and always conjugates in the same way as noun. The conjugations will be learned more in details later.

LET'S SPEAK JAPANESE 41

The difference of modification forms between noun-adjective and adjective is as follows.

    Noun-adj.   rippa na tatemono - a fine building

    Adjective   takai tatemono - a tall building

Whereas noun-adjective has to take "na" for inbetween, adjective can be used as it is in the plain form to modify noun.

It may be good to learn, at this time, some vocabularies of noun-adjective as listed below.

joozu na	skillful
heta na	unskilled
joobu na	healthy, strong
benri na	convenient
fuben na	inconvenient
rikoo na	clever
baka na	foolish
kirei na	pretty
shizuka na	quiet
daiji na	important

    Exceptional

ooki na	big
chiisa na	small

Note: These are exceptional because the regular forms are supposed to be adjectives, i.e. "ookii" and "chiisai" respectively. Only the modification form is acceptable to go like noun-adjective.

Son'na ni atarashiku arimasen.

"Son'na ni" is a popular adverb frequently used as a modifier. The literal meaning of this whole sentence is "It is not new that much." A lot of similar expressions can be made by using this adverb, such as: "Son'na ni ookiku arimasen," "Son'na ni omoshiroku arimasen," etc.

SHORT DIALOGS - MEMORIZE

Dialog 1:

A: Kon'nichi wa, Tamiya san.
B: Kon'nichi wa, Abe san no okusan.
A: Kyoo wa yoi o-tenki desu ne.
B: Ee, hontoo ni yoi o-tenki desu nee.

Dialog 2:

A: Tamiya san, are wa nan desu ka.
B: Ano rippa na tatemono desu ka. Are wa daigaku no toshokan desu yo.
A: Soo desu ka. Zuibun ookii desu nee. Atarashii desu ka.
B: Iie, son'na ni atarashiku arimasen.

DRILLS - Greetings

1. A: Kon'nichi wa Tanaka san.
   B: Kon'nichi wa Sasaki san no go-shujin.

2. A: Kon'ban wa Minami san.
   B: Kon'ban wa, Nakayama san no okusan.

   (Note: "Okusan" is used in common, but there is a word, "okusama," which is more polite.)

DRILLS - Practice of using the adjective "yoi"

1. Kyoo wa yoi o-tenki desu.   It is good weather today.
2. Kore wa yoi hon desu.   This is a good book.
3. Asoko wa yoi gakkoo desu.   That is a good school.
4. Koko wa yoi o-mise desu.   This is a good store.

DRILLS - Questions & Answers

1.
   Q: Are wa nan desu ka.
   A: Ano rippa na tatemono desu ka. Are wa machi no yuubinkyoku desu.

2.
   Q: Are wa nan desu ka.
   A: Ano ooki na tatemono desu ka. Are wa machi no byooin desu.

3.
   Q: Are wa nan desu ka.
   A: Ano kirei na hana desu ka. Are wa sakura no hana desu.

4.
   Q: Are wa nan desu ka.
   A: Ano chiisa na jidoosha desu ka. Are wa Nihon no jidoosha desu.

LET'S SPEAK JAPANESE

DRILLS - Questions & Answers

1.
   Q: Furui desu ka.
   A: Iie, son'na ni furuku arimasen.

2.
   Q: Takai desu ka.
   A: Iie, son'na ni takaku arimasen.

3.
   Q: Tooi desu ka.
   A: Iie, son'na ni tooku arimasen.

4.
   Q: Ii desu ka.
   A: Iie, son'na ni yoku arimasen.

(Note: "Ii" can be used only in case of present tense. Its conjugation is always based on "yoi." Therefore, the negative form changes to "yoku arimasen" and never to be "iku arimasen.")

EXERCISES

1. How do you say the following expressions in Japanese?

   1. What is that over there?
   2. Is that pretty building over there? That's a city library. (city = shi)
   3. It's extremely big, isn't it? Is it new?
   4. No, it's not that new.

2. Answer the questions according to the example.

   Example: Tooi desu ka.   Iie, son'na ni tooku arimasen.

   1. Yasui desu ka.
   2. Chikai desu ka.
   3. Oishii desu ka.
   4. Omoshiroi desu ka.
   5. Warui desu ka.

3. Make a situational conversation.

   One morning Mrs. Hayama meets Mr. Johnson on the street. They greet each other. Mr. Johnson wants to know what the big building in the distance is. Mrs. Hayama points to the building and tries to explain what it is. She tells that it is a bank. Now, their conversation goes on accordingly.

LET'S SPEAK JAPANESE

LESSON SIX

SUPOOTSU GA SUKI DESU KA

Yamamoto: Itsumo nani o shimasu ka.
Jonson: Taitei tenisu o shimasu.
Yamamoto: Supootsu ga suki desu ka.
Jonson: Ee, daisuki desu. Anata wa.
Yamamoto: Watashi wa amari suki ja arimasen ga, tokidoki terebi de futtobooru o mimasu.
Jonson: Futtobooru wa omoshiroi desu ne. Amerika de wa totemo popyuraa na supootsu desu.

MEANING

DO YOU LIKE SPORTS?

Yamamoto: What do you do always?
Johnson: I usually play tennis.
Yamamoto: Do you like sports?
Johnson: Yes, I like it very much. How about you?
Yamamoto: I don't like it so much, but sometimes I watch football on TV.
Johnson: Football is fun, isn't it? It's a very popular sport in America.

STRUCTURES

1. Supootsu ga suki desu ka — Nominative Supootsu + ga + noun-adjective suki + Copula desu.
2. Amari suki ja arimasen — Adverb Amari + noun-adjective suki + negative form of desu, ja arimasen
3. Amerika de wa totemo popyuraa na supootsu desu — Place noun Amerika + multiple relator particles, de wa + totemo popyuraa na supootsu desu

USEFUL EXPRESSIONS

Tokidoki terebi de futtobooru o mimasu — "Tokidoki" is one of the most frequently used adverbs meaning "sometimes." When you watch something on TV, this sort of expression is used. Especially the relator particle "de" is important to describe on what- such as on TV, over the radio, etc.

GRAMMAR GENERALIZATIONS

Itsumo nani o shimasu ka.

This means "What do you do always?" The verb "shimasu" is a general verb that represents action verbs and so, to the question as above, anything that you may do all the time can be answered.

    Itsumo nani o shimasu ka.   Toshokan de hon o yomimasu.
                                                            - I read a book at the library.

                                                           Machi de kaimono o shimasu.
                                                           - I do shopping at downtown.

                                                           Uchi de benkyoo shimasu.
                                                           - I study at home.

Taitei tenisu o shimasu.

As explained in Lesson 4, the verb "shimasu" is used in combination with all kind of sports for the English equivalent, "play."

"Taitei" is an adverb meaning "usually." Here are some similar adverbs.

    tokidoki   -   sometimes
    itsumo   -   always
    tama ni   -   rarely, once in a great while
    shibashiba   -   often, frequently
    tokiori   -   occasionally, once in a while

Supootsu ga suki desu ka.

"Suki desu" is the descriptive form of the noun-adjective meaning "is likeable." Literally this expression means "Is sport likeable?" that is, in a better expression, "Do you like sports?" "Suki" is not a verb and must be classified to be one of many noun-adjectives due to its functional nature. The descriptive form or predicate noun-adjective may be just like English adjective if translated.

    Noun-Adj.   Kono hako wa daiji desu.   This box is important.
                                  Predicate

                     Sono michi wa benri desu.   That road is convenient.
                                  Predicate

                   Sono sensei wa yuumei desu.   That teacher is famous.
                                  Predicate

All the words, "important," "convenient" and "famous," are adjectives in English, but not in Japanese.

LET'S SPEAK JAPANESE

The following are additional noun-adjectives.

majime	- serious	kawaisoo	-	pitiful, poor
fumajime	- unserious	genki	-	healthy, fine
dame	- no good	kirai	-	dislikeable
kantan	- simple	daikirai	-	dislikeable very much
tanjun	- simple-hearted	daisuki	-	likeable very much

Watashi wa amari suki ja arimasen.

"I don't like it so much." "Suki ja arimasen" is the negative form of noun-adjective. See the following conjugation.

Affirmative	Negative
Sono mise wa benri desu.	Sono mise wa benri ja arimasen.
Fujita san wa yuumei desu.	Fujita san wa yuumei ja arimasen.
Kono hana wa kirei desu.	Kono hana wa kirei ja arimasen.
Ano ko wa majime desu.	Ano ko wa majime ja arimasen.

Whereas "totemo" is used for affirmative sentence, "amari" replaces it for negative sentence.

cf. Chichi wa totemo genki desu.　　My father is very fine (healthy).
　　Chichi wa amari genki ja arimasen. My father is not too healthy.

"-Ja arimasen" can be replaced by "-de wa arimasen." The difference is that while the former is more for colloquial use, the latter is formal.

Amerika de wa (totemo popyuraa na supootsu desu)

"De wa" is a multiple relator particles. "Wa" can be used often in combination like this to bring out the preceding phrase to function as a topic of the sentence.

　　Nihon de wa,　　　　　As far as (in) Japan is concerned,
　　Gakkoo de wa,　　　　As far as (in) school is concerned,

Anata wa (supootsu ga suki desu ka)

In the course of conversation, this question apparently refers to the same topic brought by the other partner. "Anata wa" is supposed to be followed by " . . . supootsu ga suki desu ka" in turn. The latter part has been omitted by simply posing a question, "Anata wa," due to the same content.

Now, the presentation dialog does not give the structure in full, but here is an important pattern, a unique charactristic of Japanese, that should be clearly remembered.

　　　　　Anata wa supootsu ga suki desu ka.

"Wa" and "ga" combination often appears in one sentence. Both seemingly indicate subjects, but there is a clear difference between the two.

"wa" - mostly used for a topic.
"ga" - used for a more focused subject.

When these relator particles are used in a sentence, "ga" never precedes "wa" but follows the topic described with "wa" to specifically focus its subject. Example:

Kudamono wa momo ga suki desu.   As for fruits, I like peach.

There is no question about the fact that "kudamono" (fruits) is a general topic in this case and "momo" (peach) is a focused subject.

Following are some expressions with the two relator particles.

Supootsu wa yakyuu ga suki desu.	As far as sport is concerned, I like baseball.
Nihon wa aki ga ii desu.	As far as Japan is concerned autumn is good.
Tanaka san wa piano ga joozu desu.	As for Miss (Mr., Mrs.) Tanaka, she is good at piano.
Nihongo wa "te ni o ha" ga muzukashii desu.	As for Japanese language, "relator particles" are difficult. (Note: The formal relator particles are called "joshi" in grammatical terms, but Japanese often say "te ni o ha" colloquially.)

SHORT DIALOGS - MEMORIZE

DIALOG 1:

A: Itsumo nani o shimasu ka.
B: Taitei gorufu o shimasu.
A: Supootsu ga suki desu ka.
B: Ee, daisuki desu.

DIALOG 2:

A: Itsumo nani o shimasu ka.
B: Taitei pin-pon o shimasu.
A: Supootsu ga suki desu ka.
B: Ee, daisuki desu.

LET'S SPEAK JAPANESE

Practice more by using the following words.

basuketto-booru (basketball), yakyuu (baseball),
futto-booru (football), baree-booru (volley ball),
booringu (bowling), sukii (ski), sukeeto (skate)

DRILLS - Questions & Answers

A: 1. Itsumo nani o shimasu ka. Taitei joggingu o shimasu.
   2. Itsumo nani o shimasu ka. Taitei batominton o shimasu.
   3. Itsumo nani o shimasu ka. Taitei sui'ei o shimasu.
   4. Itsumo nani o shimasu ka. Taitei booringu o shimasu.

B: 1. Itsumo nani o shimasu ka. Itsumo hon o yomimasu.
   2. Itsumo nani o shimasu ka. Itsumo tegami o kakimasu.
   3. Itsumo nani o shimasu ka. Itsumo benkyoo (o) shimasu.
   4. Itsumo nani o shimasu ka. Itsumo shigoto o shimasu.

C: 1. Taitei nani o shimasu ka. Taitei terebi o mimasu.
   2. Taitei nani o shimasu ka. Taitei rajio o kikimasu.

D: 1. Tokidoki nani o shimasu ka. Tokidoki pikunikku o shimasu.
   2. Tokidoki nani o shimasu ka. Tokidoki haikingu o shimasu.
   3. Tokidoki nani o shimasu ka. Tokidoki eiga o mimasu.
   4. Tokidoki nani o shimasu ka. Tokidoki hon o yomimasu.

DRILLS - Questions & Answers

1. Supootsu ga suki desu ka. Ee, daisuki desu.
2. Dokusho ga suki desu ka. Ee, daisuki desu.
3. Benkyoo ga suki desu ka. Ee, daisuki desu.
4. Ryoori ga suki desu ka. Ee, daisuki desu.

DRILLS - Questions & Answers (Structure of "wa" and "ga" combination)

1. Anata wa ringo ga suki desu ka. Ee, suki desu yo.
2. Nihon wa natsu ga ii desu ka. Ee, ii desu yo.
3. Amerika wa tekisasu ga ookii desu ka. Ee, ookii desu yo.
4. Nihon wa aki ga kirei desu ka. Ee, kirei desu yo.

EXERCISES

1. Fill in each blank with a proper adverb.

   1. Watashi wa tenisu ga (   ) suki ja arimasen.
      (I don't like tennis too much.)

2. (   ) nani o shimasu ka.
   (What do you do sometimes?)

3. (   ) toshokan de hon o yomimasu.
   (I always read a book at the library.)

4. (   ) bifuteki o tabemasu.
   (I usually eat beef-steak.)

2. Change the following expressions to the negative form.
   1. Kume san wa genki desu.
   2. Ano michi wa benri desu.
   3. Takada san wa piano ga joozu desu.
   4. Ano hana wa kirei desu.
   5. Hirai san wa yuumei desu.
   6. Watashi wa ongaku ga suki desu.

3. Make a situational conversation between Betty (Betei) and Jack (Jakku) after reading the following narrative.

   Betty meets Jack in the afternoon. They greet each other. Betty asks Jack what he does always. Jack likes basketball very much, so he answers accordingly. Now, they talk about sports. Their conversation just goes on.

Anata wa Sumisu san desu ne.

Iie, chigaimasu.
Sumisu ja arimasen.
Jonson desu.

Iie, gakkoo ja arimasen.

Are wa gakkoo desu ka.

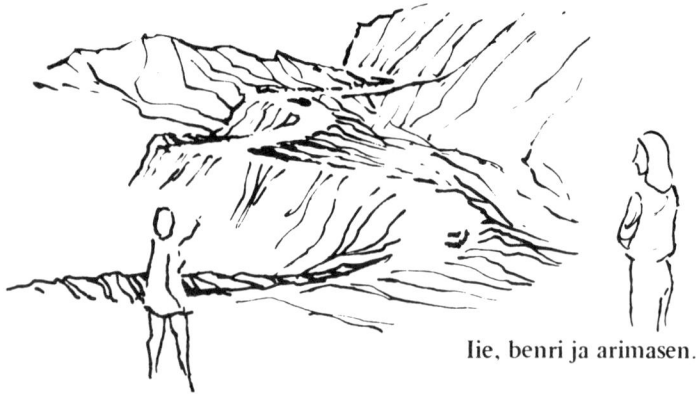

Iie, benri ja arimasen.

Sono michi wa benri desu ka.

LET'S SPEAK JAPANESE

LESSON SEVEN

HONDA JA ARIMASEN

Sasaki:	A! Anata wa Honda san desu ne.
Mishiranu Hito:	Iie, chigaimasu. Honda ja arimasen. Fujii desu.
Sasaki:	Kore wa shitsurei shimashita.
Mishiranu Hito:	Honda san nara, sakki ano koo'en ni imashita yo.
Sasaki:	A, soo desu ka. Doomo arigatoo gozaimasu.

MEANING

I AM NOT HONDA

Sasaki:	Oh, you are Mr. Honda, aren't you?
Stranger:	No, different. I am not Honda. I'm Fujii.
Sasaki:	I am sorry.
Stranger:	If (you are looking for) Mr. Honda, he was in that park a while ago.
Sasaki:	Oh, is that so? Thank you very much.

STRUCTURES

1. Honda ja arimasen	-	Proper noun + negative form of Copula, ja arimasen
2. Honda san nara	-	Proper noun + Conditional form of Copula nara
3. Ano koo'en ni imashita yo	-	Place noun + relator particle ni + past tense of imasu, imashita

USEFUL EXPRESSIONS

Iie, chigaimasu.	-	"No, it's different" or "No, I'm different." Whenever you disagree to a question which is clearly different from the fact, you can use this expression for an answer.
Kore wa shitsurei shimashita.	-	"I am sorry for what I have done." This is an apology for what has been done just now. The happening for which the apology is made must be right there between the two.

GRAMMAR GENERALIZATIONS

Honda ja arimasen.

The negative form of noun in the present tense is expressed in this pattern. This is the same pattern as used for the negative form of noun-adjective.

    cf. Noun: Yamada san wa sensei ja arimasen.
        Noun-Adj.   Sono mise wa kirei ja arimasen.

As explained in the previous lesson, the form "-ja arimasen" can be substituted by "-de wa arimasen" which is more formal. (Free variation)

Honda san nara . . .

This means "If Mr. Honda, . . . " This is a conditional form most frequently used for nouns and noun-adjectives.

"Nara" is translated "if," but it is more than that. It occurs where verbs normally occur, and might be translated "if is," or "if so." More precisely, it is the conditional form of Copula desu (da, de aru, de arimasu).

    Nouns: Sono hon nara, koko ni arimasu yo.
                   - If that book, it's over here.

                  Koohii nara, nomimasen.
                   - If coffee, I don't drink.

    Noun-Adj.   Genki nara, ii desu nee.
                   - If he (or she) is fine, it will be good.
                    (I wish he (or she) is fine.)

                  Sono michi ga benri nara, ikimasu.
                   - If that road is convenient, I will go.

Ano koo'en ni imashita yo.

The meaning of this sentence is "He was in that park." "Imashita" is the past tense or perfect tense of "imasu." All the verbs ending with -masu can be changed to -mashita for the past tense.

    Motion Verbs

    ikimasu   ikimashita
    kimasu   kimashita
    kaerimasu   kaerimashita

    Action Verbs

    tabemasu   tabemashita
    mimasu   mimashita

kakimasu	kakimashita
kikimasu	kikimashita
shimasu	shimashita

Existence Verbs

arimasu	arimashita
imasu	imashita

SHORT DIALOGS - MEMORIZE

DIALOG 1:

A: A! Anata wa Kuupaa san desu ne.
B: Iie, chigaimasu. Kuupaa ja arimasen.
A: Kore wa shitsurei shimashita.
B: Kuupaa san nara, sakki asoko ni imashita yo.
A: A, soo desu ka. Doomo arigatoo gozaimasu.

DIALOG 2:

A: A! Anata wa Toyama san desu ne.
B: Iie, chigaimasu. Toyama ja arimasen.
A: Kore wa shitsurei shimashita.
B: Toyama san nara, sakki asoko ni imashita yo.
A: A, soo desu ka. Doomo arigatoo gozaimasu.

DRILLS - Questions & Answers

1.
   Q: Anata wa Sumisu san desu ne.
   A: Iie, chigaimasu. Sumisu ja arimasen.

2.
   Q: Anata wa Hanako san desu ne.
   A: Iie, chigaimasu. Hanako ja arimasen.

3.
   Q: Anata wa Masao san desu ne.
   A: Iie, chigaimasu. Masao ja arimasen.

4.
   Q: Anata wa Katoo san desu ne.
   A: Iie, chigaimasu. Katoo ja arimasen.

DRILLS - Questions & Answers

1. Nouns

A. Q: Are wa gakkoo desu ka.
   A: Iie, gakkoo ja arimasen. Kaisha desu.

B. Q: Sore wa jimusho desu ka.
   A: Iie, jimusho ja arimasen. Omise desu.

C. Q: Kore wa jisho desu ka.
   A: Iie, jisho ja arimasen. Sankoosho desu.

D. Q: Koko wa doobutsu'en desu ka.
   A: Iie, doobutsu'en ja arimasen. Suizokukan desu.

2. Noun-Adjectives

A. Q: Kono michi wa benri desu ka.
   A: Iie, benri ja arimasen.

B. Q: Sono hana wa kirei desu ka.
   A: Iie, kirei ja arimasen.

C. Q: Ryokoo wa suki desu ka.
   A: Iie, suki ja arimasen.

D. Q: Piano wa joozu desu ka.
   A: Iie, joozu ja arimasen.

DRILLS - Conditional Form, . . . nara

1. Nouns

    1. Yamaguchi san nara, jimusho ni imasu yo.
    2. Gibuson san nara, gakkoo ni imasu yo.
    3. Takayama san nara, yuubinkyoku ni imasu yo.
    4. Kesuraa san nara, ginkoo ni imasu yo.
    * Change the above sentences to the past tense.

2. Noun-Adjectives

    1. Hontoo nara, ii desu ne.
    2. Joobu nara, ii desu ne.
    3. Byooki nara, Murata san wa kimasen yo.
    4. Genki nara, Murata san wa kimasu yo.

DRILLS - The following are very frequently used verbs. Change them to the past tense.

1.	ikimasu	(go)	9.	araimasu	(wash)
2.	kimasu	(come)	10.	nomimasu	(drink)
3.	kaerimasu	(return)	11.	kaimasu	(buy)
4.	tabemasu	(eat)	12.	urimasu	(sell)
5.	mimasu	(see, watch)	13.	haraimasu	(pay)
6.	shirabemasu	(check)	14.	hairimasu	(enter)
7.	kangaemasu	(think)	15.	kikimasu	(listen)
8.	kazoemasu	(count)	16.	hanashimasu	(talk)

LET'S SPEAK JAPANESE

17. gorufu o shimasu   (play golf)
18. benkyoo shimasu   (study)
19. shigoto (o) shimasu   (work)
20. ryoori shimasu   (cook)
21. unten shimasu   (drive)
22. kekkon shimasu   (marry)
23. ryokoo shimasu   (travel)
24. shuuri shimasu   (repair)

EXERCISES

1. Refer to the previous dialogs and make a similar dialog between two persons.

2. Change the following expressions to the negative form.
   1. Ueki san wa gakusei desu.
   2. Are wa machi no toshokan desu.
   3. Koko wa keisatsu desu.
   4. Ano hana wa bara desu.

3. Express the following sentences in the past tense.
   1. Sumisu san wa gakkoo e ikimasu.
   2. Oishii gohan o tabemasu.
   3. Kissaten de koohii o nomimasu.
   4. Jimusho ni sensei ga imasu.
   5. Uchi ni karaa terebi ga arimasu.
   6. Kimura san ga kimasu.
   7. Mainichi benkyoo shimasu.
   8. Itsumo tenisu o shimasu ka.

4. The following is a list of supplemental vocabularies. Try to make up some conversational sentences in the conditional form.

   Seiji (Politics)

Daitooryoo	- President	Kokkai	-	Congress
Fuku-daitooryoo	- Vice President	Jooin	-	House of Senate
Kokkai-gi'in	- Congress man	Kain	-	House of Representatives
Saibankan	- Judge	Shuukai	-	State Congress
Chiji	- Governor	Shikai	-	City Council
Fuku-chiji	- Lieutenant Governor	Saibansho	-	Court
Shichoo	- Mayor	seiji-ka	-	politician
Shuukai-gi'in	- State Congress man	senkyo	-	election
		toohyoo	-	vote
Shikai-gi'in	- City Council man	rikkoo-hosha	-	candidate

   Shokugyoo (Vocational)

denki	- electricity	taipisuto	-	typist
jidoosha seibi	- auto repair	hisho	-	secretary
seizu	- drafting	daiku	-	carpenter

fudoosan	- real estate	denki-koo	- electricity worker
noogyoo	- agriculture	jidoosha seibi koo	- auto repair worker
kaikei (or keiri)	- accounting	haikan-koo	- plumber
tosoo	- painting	keisatsukan	- police man
yoosetsu	- welding	toshokan'in	- librarian
bankin	- sheet metal	kukku	- cook
doboku	- engineering work	funanori	- sailor
seerusuman	- salesman	kenchikuka	- architect
ten'in	- store clerk	gaka	- artist (painter)
ginkoo'in	- bank worker	ongakuka	- musician
keirishi	- accountant	bengoshi	- attorney
kangofu	- nurse	hooritsuka	- lawyer
shihainin	- manager	ha-isha	- dentist
hoken gaikoo'in	- insurance man	isha	- medical doctor

Shuukyoo (Religions)

Kirisutokyoo	- Christianity	kyookai	- church
Bukkyoo	- Buddhism	otera	- temple (of Buddhism)
Shintoo	- Shintoism	jinja	- shrine (of Shintoism)
Yudayakyoo	- Judaism	ji'in	- Buddhist temple
Kaikyoo	- Mohammed	Katorikku-kyookai	- Catholic Church
Katorikku	- Catholic		

Ippan (General)

kikai	- machine	kisha	- train
zaimoku	- lumber	densha	- electric train
jidoosha	- automobile	chika-tetsu	- subway
hikooki	- airplane	basu	- bus
fune	- ship	takushii	- taxi.

Bunboogu (Stationeries)

hon	- book	hochikisu	- stapler
jisho	- dictionary	pen	- pen
enpitsu	- pencil	inku	- ink
man'nenhitsu	- fountain pen	enpitsu kezuri	- pencil sharpener
choomen (or nooto)	- notebook	keisanki	- calculator
nikki-choo	- diary book	koyomi (or karendaa)	- calendar
keshigomu	- eraser		

Yasai (Vegetables)

ninjin	- carrot	satsuma-imo	- sweet potato
daikon	- turnip	negi	- green onion
tomato	- tomato	tamanegi	- round onion
kabocha	- pumpkin	retasu	- lettuce

LET'S SPEAK JAPANESE

nasu	-	eggplant	hakusai	-	Chinese cabbage
kyuuri	-	cucumber	kyabetsu	-	cabbage
jagaimo	-	potato	hoorensoo	-	spinach
piiman	-	bell pepper	serori	-	celery

Kudamono (Fruits)

momo	-	peach	meron	-	melon
mikan	-	tangerine	budoo	-	grape
ringo	-	apple	banana	-	banana
nashi	-	pear	neeburu	-	navel orange
suika	-	water melon	kaki	-	persimmon

Kinoo wa ame deshita.

Kinoo wa yuki deshita.

Nihon no keizai ni tsuite hanashimashita.

Ringo wa totemo oishikatta desu.

Eiga wa totemo omoshirokatta desu.

LESSON EIGHT

TOTEMO OMOSHIROKATTA DESU YO

Sasaki: Honda san, hisashi buri deshita ne.
Honda: A, Sasaki san, itsu kochira e kimashita ka.
Sasaki: Sakki kita bakari desu. Kyoo wa ii o-tenki desu ne.
Honda: Ee. Kinoo wa ame deshita ga, kyoo wa sukkari hareagarimashita.
Sasaki: Kinoo Morita san ni aimashita ka.
Honda: Hai, aimashita. Morita san to Nihon no keizai ni tsuite iroiro hanashimashita. Totemo omoshirokatta desu yo.
Sasaki: Sore wa yokatta desu ne.

MEANING

IT WAS VERY INTERESTING TO BE SURE

Sasaki: Mr. Honda, it's been a long time to see you, hasn't it?
Honda: Oh, Mr. Sasaki, when did you come over here?
Sasaki: I just came a while ago. It's nice weather today, isn't it?
Honda: Yes. It was rainy yesterday, but it has cleared up today.
Sasaki: Did you meet Mr. Morita yesterday?
Honda: Yes, I did. I talked with him in many ways concerning Japan's economy. It was very interesting to be sure.
Sasaki: That's good.

STRUCTURES

1. Kinoo wa ame deshita — Nominative + relator particle wa + noun + past tense of Copula, deshita

2. Totemo omoshirokatta desu — Adverb totemo + past plain form of adjective + Copula desu

USEFUL EXPRESSIONS

Hisashi buri deshita ne — "It has been a long time to see you, hasn't it?" The similar expression is "Hisashi buri desu ne" meaning "It's a long time to see you, isn't it?" The difference is usage of Copula, either past tense (deshita) or present tense (desu). Interesting enough, both expressions can be used for the same situation, because "hisashi buri" indicates a long interval after the last meeting.

Sakki kita bakari desu   "I just came a while ago." As a very useful expression just memorize this through mimicry, because here is a new verbal form, kita, which you have not learned yet. It is the plain past tense of the irregular verb, kimasu.

"Sakki" means a while ago.

GRAMMAR GENERALIZATIONS

Itsu kochira e kimashita ka.

"Itsu" is an interrogative word meaning "when." "Kochira" means "over here." There are similar words which indicate locations.

1.	koko	here
	soko	there
	asoko	over there
2.	kochira	over here
	sochira	over there
	achira	over that place

The words in the group 2 are more polite than the words in the group 1.

Kinoo wa ame deshita.

"Ame" is a noun in Japanese. The sentence literally means "Yesterday was rain." It may be funny, but this sort of expression stands in Japanese. Needless to say, better expression in English is "It was rainy yesterday."

To express something in the past tense, the Copula must be changed to deshita from desu. Again, nouns and noun-adjectives take the same pattern for the past tense.

	Present Tense	Past Tense
Noun:	Yamada san wa sensei desu.	Yamada san wa sensei deshita.
	Gakkoo wa soko desu.	Gakkoo wa soko deshita.
Noun-Adj:	Sono michi wa benri desu.	Sono michi wa benri deshita.
	Otooto wa uta ga heta desu.	Otooto wa uta ga heta deshita.

Totemo omoshirokatta desu yo.

"It was very interesting to be sure." The past tense of adjective is a unique form. As noted previously, all the adjectives end with -i after the following vowels which either come up as they are or in combination with consonant like ka, shi, ru, ro, etc.

The following are some examples.

a	akai	(red)		
i	kawaii	(cute)	oishii	(delicious)
u	monoui	(weary)	warui	(bad)
e	There is no combination with this vowel.			
o	aoi	(blue)	sugoi	(terrific)

Now, it is a characteristic of adjectives that all the final -i must be completely dropped off to be replaced by -katta for the past tense. For example:

Present Tense	Past Tense
Kono ringo wa oishii desu.	Kono ringo wa oishikatta desu.
(This apple is delicious.)	(This apple was delicious.)

Don't let the final -i sound at all when you drop it off to pronounce the adjective in the past tense.

Kono ringo wa oishikatta desu. - Correct
Kono ringo wa oishiikatta desu. - Wrong

Sometimes the past tense is described simply as "Kono ringo wa oishii deshita" without changing the final -i and by using the past tense of Copula, deshita. However, since the adjectives conjugate with elimination of the final -i for negative form, conditional form, etc., let us remember the katta form for the adjective past tense.

SHORT DIALOGS - MEMORIZE

DIALOG 1:

A: Baba san, hisashi buri desu ne.
B: A, Abe san. Itsu kochira e kimashita ka.
A: Kinoo kita bakari desu.
B: Aa, soo desu ka.

DIALOG 2:

A: Kinoo Yano san ni aimashita ka.
B: Hai, aimashita. Yano san to Nippon no shakai ni tsuite iroiro hanashimashita. Totemo omoshirokatta desu yo.
A: Sore wa yokatta desu ne.

DRILLS

A. Questions & Answers

1. Itsu kochira e kimashita ka.   Kinoo kimashita.
2. Itsu sochira e ikimashita ka.   Kyonen ikimashita.
3. Itsu achira e ikimashita ka.   Senshuu ikimashita.
4. Itsu Nihon e kaerimashita ka.   Sen'getsu kaerimashita.

(It may be hard to judge who came or who went. It may be you or somebody else. Japanese people often skip the subject if they mutually understand it. In case you want to specifically indicate somebody, you just mention him or her with the topic relator particle wa. Example: "Sumisu san wa itsu kochira e kimashita ka."

B: The following are supplemental vocabularies for practice. Say something by using the idiomatic relator particle, ... ni tsuite.

Example: shakai (society) - Nihon no shakai ni tsuite hanashimashita.

1. roodoo kumiai (labor union)
2. shakai mondai (social problem)
3. kyooiku (education)
4. seiji (politics)
5. sekai mondai (world problem)
6. seifu (government)
7. ningen kankei (human relationship)
8 seikatsu (life, livelihood)

C: Express the following sentences in the past tense.

Verbs

1.	Uchi e kaerimasu.	Uchi e kaerimashita.
2.	Gohan o tabemasu.	Gohan o tabemashita.
3.	Koohii o nomimasu.	Koohii o nomimashita.
4.	Jimusho ni sensei ga imasu.	Jimusho ni sensei ga imashita.
5.	Kono machi ni byooin ga arimasu ka.	Kono machi ni byooin ga arimashita ka.
6.	Gakkoo e kimasu ka.	Gakkoo e kimashita ka.
7.	Mainichi benkyoo shimasu ka.	Mainichi benkyoo shimashita. ka.
8.	Itsumo gorufu o shimasu.	Itsumo gorufu o shimashita.

Adjectives

1.	Kono nashi wa oishii desu yo.	Kono nashi wa oishikatta desu yo.
2.	San Furanshisuko wa tooi desu.	San Furanshisuko wa tookatta desu.
3.	Ano mise wa takai desu.	Ano mise wa takakatta desu.
4.	Furansugo wa yasashii desu ka.	Furansugo wa yasashikatta desu ka.
5.	Soko wa abunai desu.	Soko wa abunakatta desu.
6.	Sono eiga wa tsumaranai desu.	Sono eiga wa tsumaranakatta desu.
7.	Honoruru wa atatakai desu.	Honoruru wa atatakakatta desu.
8.	Arasuka wa samui desu.	Arasuka wa samukatta desu.

Noun-Adjectives (Prestudy - More Details in Lesson 9)

1.	Ano koo'en wa shizuka desu.	Ano koo'en wa shizuka deshita.
2.	Suzuki san wa yuumei desu.	Suzuki san wa yuumei deshita.
3.	Kono michi wa fuben desu yo.	Kono michi wa fuben deshita yo.

LET'S SPEAK JAPANESE

4. Supootsu wa suki desu ka. — Supootsu wa suki deshita ka.
5. Chichi wa byooki desu. — Chichi wa byooki deshita.
6. Sono gakkoo wa rippa desu. — Sono gakkoo wa rippa deshita.
7. Ano kata wa joohin desu. — Ano kata wa joohin deshita.
8. Akiko san wa majime desu. — Akiko san wa majime deshita.

Nouns

1. Sawamura san wa sensei desu. — Sawamura san wa sensei deshita.
2. Watakushi wa gakusei desu. — Watakushi wa gakusei deshita.
3. Horita san wa isha desu. — Horita san wa isha deshita.
4. Asoko wa gakkoo desu. — Asoko wa gakkoo deshita.
5. Koko wa byooin desu. — Koko wa byooin deshita.
6. Uchi wa Shikago desu. — Uchi wa Shikago deshita.
7. Kore wa jimusho desu. — Kore wa jimusho deshita.
8. Soko wa kaisha desu. — Soko wa kaisha deshita.

EXERCISES

1. Make questions with the interrogative word, "itsu."

   Example:
   When did you come over here?   Itsu kochira e kimashita ka.

   1. When did you go over there?
   2. When did you return home?
   3. When did you return to Japan?
   4. When did you come to this town?
   5. When did you eat dinner?
   6. When did you play golf?
   7. When did you buy the car?

2. Complete the following conversation.

   A: Morita san, _____
      It has been long to see you, hasn't it?

   B: A, Yasuda san. _____
      When did you come over here?

   A: _____   Kyoo wa ii o-tenki desu ne.
      I just came a while ago.

   B: Ee._____ga, kyoo wa sukkari hareagarimashita.
      It was rainy yesterday.

3. Express the following sentences in Japanese.

   1. The movie was very interesting.
   2. Is Denver far?
   3. No, it is not far.
   4. I guess it must probably be near.
   5. Was the apple delicious?

Minasan, kon'ban wa.
Watakushi no namae wa Teiraa Jooji desu.
Mae wa seerusuman deshita ga, ima wa shikai-gi'in desu.

Mukashi wa ryokoo ga totemo suki deshita.
Demo, ima wa amari suki ja arimasen.

LESSON NINE

This lesson is a short speech designed to help you develop skills of expressing yourself based on a certain situation. Even two or three lines of expressions are a good start if you can. Study the lesson carefully and practice to express yourself in your own words.

SUPIICHI

Minasan, Kon'nichi wa. Watakushi no namae wa Shimizu Ichiroo desu. Mae wa sensei deshita ga, ima wa bijinesuman desu. Mukashi wa eiga ga totemo suki deshita. Demo, ima wa amari suki ja arimasen. Tokidoki, machi no toshokan e ikimasu. Mochiron, daigaku no toshokan e mo tama ni ikimasu. Gan ni tsuite, kono mae, hon o yomimashita. Taihen tame ni narimashita. Anata mo sono hon o yomimasen ka.

MEANING

SPEECH

Good afternoon, everyone. My name is Ichiro Shimizu. I was a teacher before, but I am a businessman now. I liked movie before (or long ago). But, I don't like it too much now. Sometimes I go to the library in town. Of course, I go to the university library once in a while, too. I read a book about cancer the other day. It was very helpful. Won't you read the book, too?

STRUCTURES

1.	Mae wa sensei deshita	-	Time noun + wa + noun + past tense of Copula, deshita
2.	Totemo suki deshita	-	Adverb + noun-adjective suki + past tense of Copula, deshita
3.	Daigaku no toshokan e mo ikimasu	-	Place noun + goal movement relator particle e + relator particle mo + motion verb, ikimasu
4.	Tame ni narimashita	-	Complement + relator particle ni + verb narimashita
5.	Anata mo sono hon o yomimasen ka		Pronoun + relator particle mo + object + relator particle o + negative form of verb yomimasen + ending particle ka for a question

USEFUL EXPRESSIONS

Minasan, kon'nichi wa — "Good afternoon, everyone." When you talk or address a group of people, often the word, "minasan" or "minasama" is used as meaning "everyone." Needless to say, if it is morning time, the greeting changes to "Ohayoo gozaimasu" and if evening or night time, "Kon'ban wa" respectively.

GRAMMAR GENERALIZATIONS

Mae wa sensei deshita.

The past tense of Copula used for noun is "deshita." Therefore, the meaning of this sentence is "I was a teacher before." Compare the following two sentences.

Yamada san wa sensei desu.	Mr. Yamada is a teacher.
Yamada san wa sensei deshita.	Mr. Yamada was a teacher.

Totemo suki deshita.

"Suki" is classified under noun-adjective group which is different from adjectives due to its conjugation. Noun-adjectival words change in the same form as nouns for the past tense.

cf.	Denbaa ga suki desu.	I like Denver. (Lit. Denver is likeable.)
	Denbaa ga suki deshita.	I liked Denver. (Lit. Denver was likeable.)

All the noun adjectives conjugate as mentioned above in the same way as nouns all the time, except in case they are of modification form like "kirei na hana" that means "pretty flower."

Daigaku no toshokan e mo ikimasu.

The combination of two relator particles, e and mo, is a pattern of multiple usage of relator particles. "Mo" functions as "also" to emphasize the statement "I am going to the university library, too." The combination of this "mo" with other relator particle connotes "even." Therefore, the above statement could be "I am going even to the library." "Mo" can be used in replacement of "e," if you want, like "Daigaku no toshokan mo ikimasu," but in this case the statement is less emphatic about the goal movement.

There are quite a few combinations with this relator particle, "mo," while

LET'S SPEAK JAPANESE   69

it is often used alone in lieu of other relator particles to make up the meaning, "also" or "too." Examples:

    Gakkoo e mo ikimashita.   Gakkoo mo ikimashita.
    Ringo o mo tabemashita.   Ringo mo tabemashita.

In a certain case, however, it doesn't work unless otherwise in the multiple combination to function for the meaning.

Chaina Taun de mo tabemashita. Never be: Chaina Taun mo tabemashita.
(I ate also at China Town.)   (Lit. I also ate China Town.)

Tame ni narimashita.

"It was helpful to me." (Lit. It became beneficial.) This is a typical form composing the meaning, "... has become ..." or "... became ..." by taking either noun or noun-adjective as complement in combination with ni. "Tame" literally means "benefit."

    Nouns   Yamada san wa sensei ni narimashita.
                Mr. Yamada became a teacher.

                Sumisu san wa shichoo ni narimashita.
                Mr. Smith became Mayor.

    Noun-Adj. Yamada san wa piano ga joozu ni narimashita.
                Mr. Yamada became skillful at piano.

                Sumisu san wa yuumei ni narimashita.
                Mr. Smith became famous.

NOTE: Don't get confused with the adjective form on this. The final -i of adjective has to be dropped off and replaced by ku to be immediately followed by "narimashita." Refer to the following example.

    Banana wa yasui desu.   Banana is inexpensive.
    Banana wa yasuku narimashita. Banana became inexpensive.

Anata mo sono hon o yomimasen ka.

This presents a pattern of the expression asking for a listener's or second person's will to do something, like the English equivalent, "Won't you do ...?" form. "Yomimasu ka" is a regular affirmative question meaning "Do you read?" or "Are you going to read?", but if a question is made from the first person to the second person in the negative form like "Yomimasen ka," the meaning will be "Won't you read?"

Here are some examples.

    Gohan o tabemasu ka.   Gohan o tabemasen ka.

- Do you eat meal?	- Won't you eat meal?
Koohii o nomimasu ka. - Do you drink coffee?	Koohii o nomimasen ka. - Won't you drink coffee?
Ashita koko ni kimasu ka. - Are you coming here tomorrow?	Ashita koko ni kimasen ka. - Won't you come here tomorrow?
Tenisu o shimasu ka. - Do you play tennis?	Tenisu o shimasen ka. - Won't you play tennis?

SPEECH 1:

Minasan, Ohayoo gozaimasu. Watakushi no namae wa Sasaki Kimiko desu. Mae wa depaato no ten'in deshita ga, ima wa kaisha no hisho desu. Mukashi wa dokusho ga suki deshita. Demo, ima wa amari suki ja arimasen. Tokidoki machi no koo'en e ikimasu. Mochiron, biichi e mo tama ni ikimasu. Nihon no niwa ni tsuite, kono mae, zasshi o yomimashita. Taihen tame ni narimashita. Anata mo sono hon o yomimasen ka.

Vocabularies

ten'in	- sales clerk		koo'en	- park
kaisha	- company		biichi	- beach
hisho	- secretary		niwa	- garden, yard
dokusho	- reading books			

SPEECH 2

Minasan, kon'ban wa. Watakushi no namae wa Jeemusu Ruisu desu. Mae wa jidoosha no shuuri-koo deshita ga, ima wa gasorin sutando no keieisha desu. Mukashi wa jidoosha ga suki ja arimasen deshita. Demo, ima wa dai-suki desu. Tokidoki inaka no hoo e ikimasu. Mochiron, Rosanzerusu e mo tama ni ikimasu. Enjin ni tsuite, kono mae, hon o yomimashita. Taihen tame ni narimashita. Anata mo sono hon o yomimasen ka.

Vocabularies

Jeemusu Ruisu	-	James Louis
jidoosha (no) shuuri-koo	-	automobile repair man
gasorin sutando	-	gasoline station
keieisha	-	manager, operator
inaka no hoo	-	country side
Rosanzerusu	-	Los Angeles
enjin	-	engine

LET'S SPEAK JAPANESE

DRILLS - Questions & Answers

A:

1. Mukashi wa nani ga suki deshita ka.   Eiga ga totemo suki deshita.
2. Mukashi wa nani ga kirai deshita ka.   Sakana ga kirai deshita.
3. Mukashi wa nani ga joozu deshita ka.   Suiei ga joozu deshita.
4. Mukashi wa nani ga heta deshita ka.   Piano ga heta deshita.

B:

1. Mae wa nan deshita ka.   Mae wa sensei deshita.
2. Mae wa nan deshita ka.   Mae wa gakusei deshita.
3. Mae wa nan deshita ka.   Mae wa ten'in deshita.
4. Mae wa nan deshita ka.   Mae wa bijinesuman deshita.

DRILLS - Present Tense & Past Tense of Noun-Adjectives

1. Kono hako wa benri desu.   Kono hako wa benri deshita.
2. Sono michi wa fuben desu.   Sono michi wa fuben deshita.
3. Kukku san wa yuumei desu.   Kukku san wa yuumei deshita.
4. Chichi wa byooki desu.   Chichi wa byooki deshita.
5. Ojisan wa genki desu.   Ojisan wa genki deshita.
6. Sono hana wa kirei desu.   Sono hana wa kirei deshita.

Use the following words and express in the past tense.

rippa	-	splendid
gooka	-	gorgeous
shizuka	-	quiet
suki	-	likeable
kirai	-	dislikeable
joobu	-	strong, sturdy
taisetsu	-	important
kantan	-	simple
kisaku	-	open-hearted
shinsen	-	fresh
namaiki	-	sassy
ubu	-	naive

DRILLS - Present Tense & Past Tense of Nouns

1. Watakushi wa gakusei desu.   Watakushi wa gakusei deshita.
2. Hanako san wa pianisuto desu.   Hanako san wa pianisuto deshita.
3. Kazuo san wa untenshu desu.   Kazuo san wa untenshu deshita.
4. Betei san wa ginkoo'in desu.   Betei san wa ginkoo'in deshita.
5. Kume san wa shachoo desu.   Kume san wa shachoo deshita.
6. Jooji san wa yakyuu no senshu desu.   Jooji san wa yakyuu no senshu deshita.

Use the following words and express in the past tense.

daiku	-	carpenter	gaka	-	artist (painter)
gishi	-	engineer	on'gakuka	-	musician
kyooju	-	professor	seijika	-	politician
joshu	-	assistant	niwashi	-	garden designer

DRILLS - Multiple Relator Particles

A: e + mo

1. Daigaku e ikimasu. — Daigaku e mo ikimasu.
2. Shikago e ikimasu. — Shikago e mo ikimasu.
3. Koko e kimasu. — Koko e mo kimasu.
4. Uchi e kaerimasu. — Uchi e mo kaerimasu.

B: o + mo

1. Gohan o tabemashita. — Gohan o mo tabemashita.
2. Hon o kaimashita. — Hon o mo kaimashita.
3. Koohii o nomimashita. — Koohii o mo nomimashita.
4. Yakyuu o shimashita. — Yakyuu o mo shimashita.

C: ni + mo

1. Ookii koo'en wa Nyuu Yooku ni arimasu. — Ookii koo'en wa Nyuu Yooku ni mo arimasu.
2. Gakkoo wa machi ni arimasu. — Gakkoo wa machi ni mo arimasu.
3. Yama wa Hawai ni arimasu. — Yama wa Hawai ni mo arimasu.
4. Ike wa koo'en ni arimasu. — Ike wa koo'en ni mo arimasu.

D: de + mo

1. Suehiro de o-sushi o tabemashita. — Suehiro de mo o-sushi o tabemashita.
2. Shokudoo de biiru o nomimashita. — Shokudoo de mo biiru o nomimashita.
3. Dezunii Rando de asobimashita. — Dezunii Rando de mo asobimashita.
4. Toshokan de benkyoo shimashita. — Toshokan de mo benkyoo shimashita.

EXERCISES

1. Express the following sentences in Japanese.

    Example: Mr. Ford became the President.
    Foodo san wa Daitooryoo ni narimashita.

    A: 1. Mr. Tanada became a teacher.
       2. Miss Kawano became a pianist.

3. Mr. Kessler became a politician.
4. Miss Carlson became a secretary.
5. Miss Kinoshita became an artist.

B: 1. The flower became pretty.
2. The road became convenient.
3. Jack became skillful at the piano.
4. The town became quiet.
5. Mr. Johnson became famous.

2. Change the following expressions to the past tense.
   1. Watakushi wa hisho desu.
   2. Sono jidoosha wa suki desu.
   3. Buraun san wa kyooju desu.
   4. Haha wa genki desu.
   5. Ano hoteru wa gooka desu.
   6. Doko e ikimasu ka.
   7. Seinto Ruisu wa tooi desu.
   8. Mainichi miruku o nomimasu.
   9. Yama wa kirai desu.
   10. Sono hana wa kirei desu.

3. Write a speech about yourself and memorize it to make a presentation in the class.

"Kinoo no shinbun o yomimashita ka."

"Iie, yomimasen deshita."

Sutoraiki wa nakereba ii desu ne.

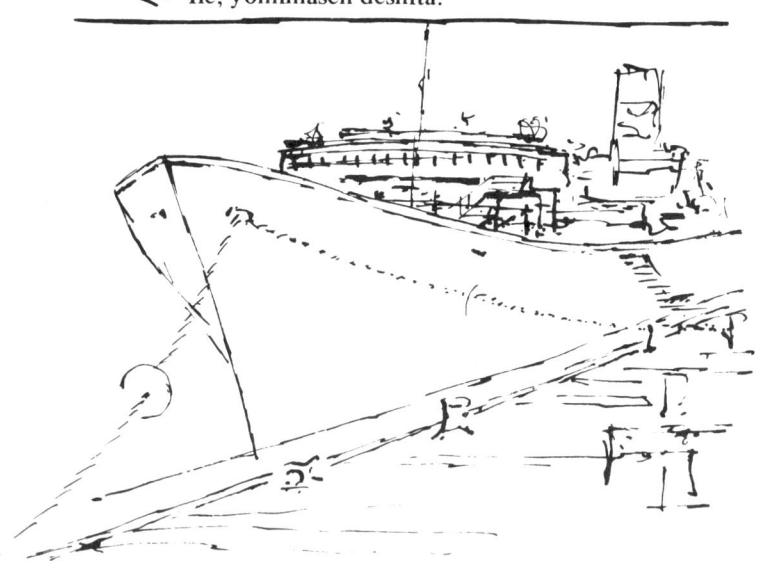

Tabun-nagai kamo shiremasen.

LET'S SPEAK JAPANESE 75

LESSON TEN

DONNA NYUUSU DESHITA KA

- (1) -

Yamamoto:	Kinoo no nyuusu o kikimashita ka.
Takahashi:	Iie, kikimasen deshita. Donna nyuusu deshita ka.
Yamamoto:	Son'na ni ooki na nyuusu ja arimasen deshita ga, rei no sutoraiki desu yo.
Takahashi:	Aa, are desu ka. Sutoraiki wa nakereba ii desu ne.

- (2) -

Yamamoto:	Tootoo sutoraiki ni narimashita ne.
Takahashi:	Kyonen wa nagakatta desu ka.
Yamamoto:	Iie, amari nagaku wa arimasen deshita.
Takahashi:	Kotoshi wa doo deshoo ka.
Yamamoto:	Saa, tabun nagai kamo shiremasen ne.

MEANING
WHAT KIND OF NEWS WAS THAT?

- (1) -

Yamamoto:	Did you listen to the yesterday's news?
Takahashi:	No, I didn't. What kind of news was that?
Yamamoto:	It wasn't that big news, but it's about that strike, you know.
Takahashi:	Oh, you mean that. I wish there won't be the strike.

- (2) -

Yamamoto:	They've finally got in a strike, haven't they?
Takahashi:	Was it long last year?
Yamamoto:	No, it was not too long.
Takahashi:	I wonder how it is going to be this year.
Yamamoto:	Well, it might probably be long.

STRUCTURES

1.	Kinoo no nyuusu o kikimashita ka.	-	Object + o + verbal past tense + ka
2.	Kikimasen deshita	-	Negative past tense of verb
3.	Donna nyuusu deshita ka	-	Interrogative word, donna + noun + past tense of Copula + ka
4.	Son'na ni ooki na nyuusu ja arimasen deshita	-	Noun + negative past tense of Copula
5.	Nagakatta desu ka	-	Plain past tense of adjective + Copula + ka
6.	Amari nagaku wa arimasen deshita	-	Adverb + negative past tense of adjective
7.	Nagai kamo shiremasen	-	Plain adjective + kamo shiremasen

USEFUL EXPRESSIONS

Sutoraiki wa nakereba ii desu ne. — "I wish there won't be a strike." "Nakereba" literally means "if there is none."

Doo deshoo ka. — "I wonder how (or what) it is going to be."

GRAMMAR GENERALIZATIONS

Kinoo no nyuusu o kikimashita ka.

The past tense of "-masu" form of verb is "-mashita." Therefore, this whole sentence simply means "Did you listen to the yesterday's news?" The following are some verbs for your reference both in the present tense and past tense.

ikimasu	ikimashita
kaerimasu	kaerimashita
kimasu	kimashita
arimasu	arimashita
imasu	imashita
tabemasu	tabemashita
shirabemasu	shirabemashita
nomimasu	nomimashita
kaimasu	kaimashita
shimasu	shimashita
yarimasu	yarimashita

The past tense can be easily formed by changing -masu to -mashita.

Kikimasen deshita.

This is a pattern of negative past tense of verb in the polite form. The pattern consists of two basic forms, that is, the negative present tense of verb plus the past tense of Copula. Refer to the following examples to see how they work.

Negative Present Tense	Negative Past Tense
ikimasen	ikimasen deshita
kaerimasen	kaerimasen deshita
kimasen	kimasen deshita
arimasen	arimasen deshita
imasen	imasen deshita

tabemasen	tabemasen deshita
shirabemasen	shirabemasen deshita
nomimasen	nomimasen deshita
kaimasen	kaimasen deshita
shimasen	shimasen deshita
yarimasen	yarimasen deshita

All you have to do is to add "deshita" to the negative present tense.

NOTE: There is one other pattern of verbal negative past tense that conjugates from -nai form to -nakatta. This is the plain form of the negative and sounds less polite than -masen deshita. Since this conjugation is different, depending on vowel verbs, consonant verbs and irregular verbs, it is a little complicated and should be learned at more advanced level. Just for your reference, however, are some examples below.

Vowel Verb

tabenai desu	tabenakatta desu
shirabenai desu	shirabenakatta desu

Consonant Verb

nomanai desu	nomanakatta desu
kawanai desu	kawanakatta desu

Irregular Verb

konai desu	konakatta desu
shinai desu	shinakatta desu

Donna nyuusu deshita ka.

"Donna" means "What kind of" to function as an interrogative word to modify somebody or something immediately.

Donna hito desu ka.	What kind of person is he?
Donna inu desu ka.	What kind of dog is it?
Donna kudamono desu ka.	What kind of fruit is it?
Donna hito deshita ka.	What kind of person was he?
Donna ushi deshita ka.	What kind of cattle was it?
Donna machi deshita ka.	What kind of town was it?

"Donna" cannot be used alone without modifying a word.

Son'na ni ooki na nyuusu ja arimasen deshita.

"It was not that big news." The negative past tense of noun is decided by putting "deshita" at the end of the present negative form. It is the same pattern as the negative past tense of noun adjectives.

	Negative Present Tense	Negative Past Tense
Noun	Gakkoo ja arimasen.	Gakkoo ja arimasen deshita.
Noun-Adj.	Kirei ja arimasen.	Kirei ja arimasen deshita.

Nagakatta desu ka & Amari nagaku wa arimasen deshita:

"Was it long?" and "It was not too long." One charactristic of adjectives is the way they change to form a negative structure and past tense structure. In case of the negative structure, the final -i changes to -ku, and is then followed by arimasen for the present tense or arimasen deshita for the past tense. The native Japanese often say "nagaku wa arimasen" to state more clearly about the fact of its negative part or even emphasize it. Either form with wa or without wa is acceptable.

In case of the past tense, the final -i must change to -katta, and is then followed by desu. "-Katta" indicates the past tense, and so there is no need to change Copula to deshita from desu.

The following is the example to show how the adjective has to conjugate.

Sutoraiki wa nagai desu.	The strike is long.
Sutoraiki wa nagaku arimasen.	The strike is not long.
Sutoraiki wa nagakatta desu.	The strike was long.
Sutoraiki wa nagaku arimasen deshita.	The strike was not long.

The last two sentences are the new patterns on this lesson.

You must have noticed that all the negative past tense of verbs, adjectives, nouns and noun-adjectives can be formed by adding deshita to their negative present tense.

	Negative Present	Negative Past
Verb:	ikimasen	ikimasen deshita
Adjective:	oishiku arimasen	oishiku arimasen deshita
Noun:	gakusei ja arimasen	gakusei ja arimasen deshita
Noun-Adj:	joozu ja arimasen	joozu ja arimasen deshita

Nagai kamo shiremasen.

"-Kamo shiremasen" is just like the English equivalent, "-might be-." As an idiomatic pattern, it may be wise to memorize the form as being connected immediately with plain form of adjective.

LET'S SPEAK JAPANESE

Oishii kamo shiremasen.	It might be delicious.
Tanoshii kamo shiremasen.	It might be fun.
Takai kamo shiremasen.	It might be expensive.
Chikai kamo shiremasen.	It might be close.
Akai kamo shiremasen.	It might be red.

Incidentally, the same form can be applied to verbs, nouns and noun-adjectives as follows.

Verb:	Yamada san wa iku kamo shiremasen.	Mr. Yamada might go.
Noun:	Yamada san wa gakusei kamo shiremasen.	Mr. Yamada might be a student.
Noun-Adj:	Yamada san wa piano ga joozu kamo shiremasen.	Mr. Yamada might be skillful at the piano.

SHORT DIALOGS - MEMORIZE

DIALOG 1:

A: Kinoo no shinbun o yomimashita ka.
B: Iie, yomimasen deshita. Donna kiji deshita ka.
A: Son'na ni ooki na kiji ja arimasen deshita ga, rei no shiken desu yo.
B: Aa, are desu ka. Shiken wa nakereba ii desu ne.

DIALOG 2:

A: Tootoo shiken ni narimashita ne.
B: Kyonen wa muzukashikatta desu ka.
A: Iie, amari muzukashiku wa arimasen deshita.
B: Kotoshi wa doo deshoo ka.
A: Saa, tabun muzukashii kamo shiremasen ne.

DRILLS - Questions & Answers

A:
1. Kinoo no rajio o kikimashitaka.   Iie, kikimasen deshita.
2. Senshuu no zasshi o yomimashita ka.   Iie, yomimasen deshita.
3. Tamura san no shashin o mimashita ka.   Iie, mimasen deshita.
4. Seeru no shatsu o kaimashita ka.   Iie, kaimasen deshita.
5. Nihon no sukiyaki o tabemashita ka.   Iie, tabemasen deshita.

B:
1. Donna nyuusu deshita ka.   Sonna ni ooki na nyuusu ja arimasen deshita ga, rei no eiga desu yo.
2. Donna hana deshita ka.   Sonna ni kirei na hana ja arimasen deshita ga, rei no bara desu yo.

3. Donna hito deshita ka. — Sonna ni hansamu na hito ja arimasen deshita ga, rei no otoko desu yo.
4. Donna tokoro deshita ka. — Sonna ni rippa na tokoro ja arimasen deshita ga, rei no machi desu yo.
5. Donna hanashi deshita ka. — Sonna ni ii hanashi ja arimasen deshita ga, rei no mondai desu yo.

C: 1. Eiga wa nagakatta desu ka. — Iie, amari nagaku arimasen deshita.
2. Osushi wa oishikatta desu ka. — Iie, amari oishiku arimasen deshita.
3. Sono shoosetsu wa omoshirokatta desu ka. — Iie, amari omoshiroku arimasen deshita.
4. Pikunikku wa tanoshikatta desu ka. — Iie, amari tanoshiku arimasen deshita.
5. Tenki wa yokatta desu ka. — Iie, amari yoku arimasen deshita.
6. Gakkoo wa tookatta desu ka. — Iie, amari tooku arimasen deshita.
7. Hoteru wa yasukatta desu ka. — Iie, amari yasuku arimasen deshita.
8. Shima wa ookikatta desu ka. — Iie, amari ookiku arimasen deshita.

DRILLS

1. Furorida wa tooi desu. — Furorida wa tooi kamo shiremasen.
2. Tekisasu wa ookii desu. — Tekisasu wa ookii kamo shiremasen.
3. Ryokoo wa tanoshii desu. — Ryokoo wa tanoshii kamo shiremasen.
4. Suika wa yasui desu. — Suika wa yasui kamo shiremasen.
5. Sono jidoosha wa furui desu. — Sono jidoosha wa furui kamo shiremasen.
6. Sensei wa isogashii desu. — Sensei wa isogashii kamo shiremasen.
7. Sono daigaku wa ii desu. — Sono daigaku wa ii kamo shiremasen.
8. Honoruru wa atatakai desu. — Honoruru wa atatakai kamo shiremasen.

LET'S SPEAK JAPANESE
EXERCISES

1. Change the following expressions to the negative past tense.

    1. Kinoo Tookyoo e ikimashita.
    2. Shikago wa tookatta desu.
    3. Watakushi wa mae sensei deshita.
    4. Kono machi wa mukashi shizuka deshita.
    5. Mainichi benkyoo shimasu.
    6. Sono ringo wa oishii desu.
    7. Asoko wa gakkoo desu.
    8. Hayama sensei wa yuumei desu.

2. Express the following in Japanese.

    1. Did you read the magazine of the last week?
    2. No, I did not read it.
    3. What kind of article was that?
    4. It was not that interesting article.

3. Make a short dialog between two persons on the topic, "Taifuu" (Typhoon) or "Jishin" (Earthquake).

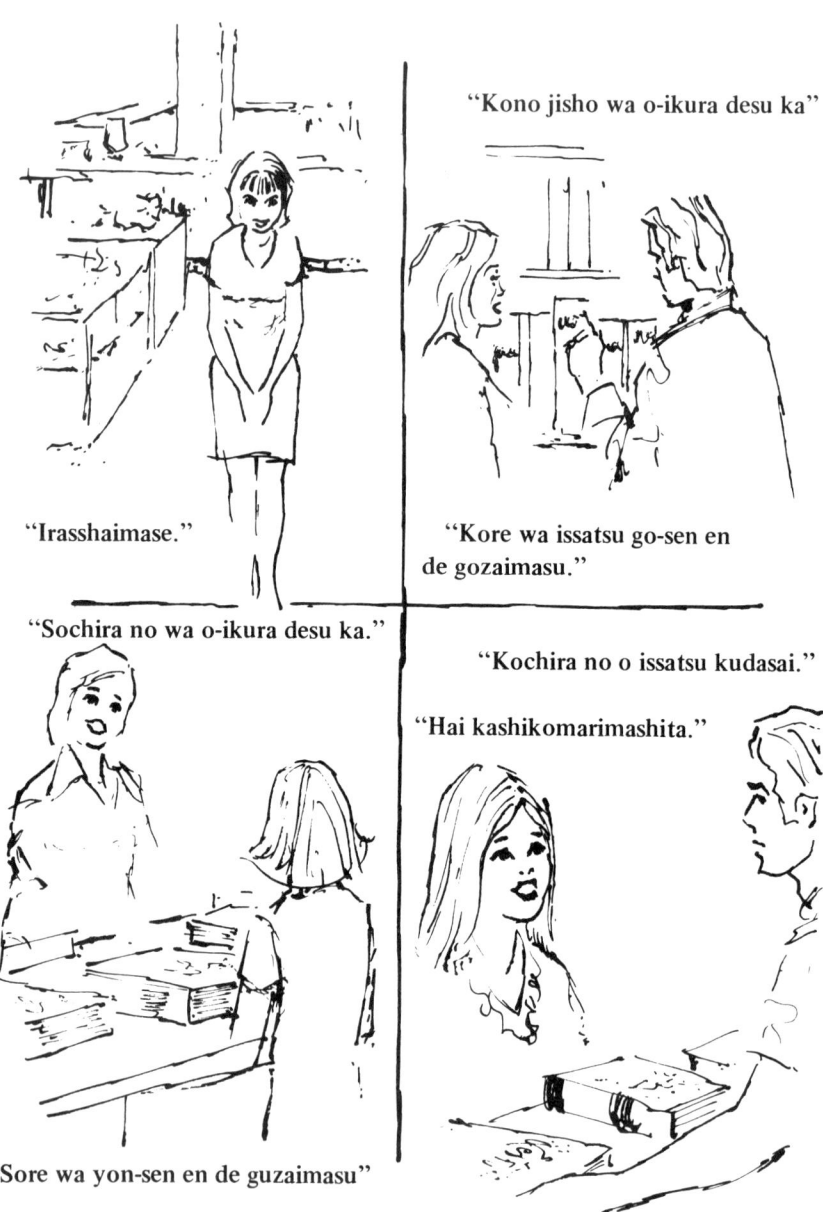

LET'S SPEAK JAPANESE

LESSON ELEVEN

SOCHIRA NO WA O-IKURA DESU KA

Ten'in:	Irasshaimase.
Hanako:	Kono man'nenhitsu wa ippon o-ikura desu ka.
Ten'in:	Kore de gozaimasu ka. Kore wa ippon yon-sen en de gozaimasu.
Hanako:	Sochira no wa o-ikura desu ka.
Ten'in:	Sore wa go-sen en de gozaimasu.
Hanako:	Sore dewa, kochira no o ippon kudasai.
Ten'in:	Hai, kashikomarimashita.

MEANING

Sales Clerk:	Welcome to the store.
Hanako:	How much is this fountain pen?
Sales Clerk:	You mean this? This is ¥ 4,000 a piece.
Hanako:	How much is the one there?
Sales Clerk:	That is ¥ 5,000.
Hanako:	Well then, give me this one.
Sales Clerk:	Certainly.

USEFUL EXPRESSIONS

Irasshaimase.	- "Welcome to the store.", "Welcome here.", "Welcome to the restaurant.", etc. This is the expression used by a host or hostess of the store, restaurant, hotel, etc. to a customer.
Kashikomarimashita.	- "Certainly." "I understood." Usually, when something is ordered a host or hostess or sales clerk uses this expression.

STRUCTURES

1. Kore wa ippon yon-sen en de gozaimasu — Nominative + counter + complement + polite form of Copula, de gozaimasu

2. Sochira no wa o-ikura desu ka — Possessive pronoun, Sochira no + wa + interrogative word, o-ikura + desu ka

GRAMMAR GENERALIZATIONS

Kore wa ippon yon-sen en de gozaimasu.

There are two things that have to be noted here. One is a counter of a thing that has to be classified clearly. Ippon is a combination of ichi and classifier, hon, which is used for identity of slim and long item like fountain-pen, pencil, umbrella, neck-tie, bamboo pole, etc. To pronounce it easier, Japanese people call it "ippon" instead of "ichi hon."

The counter can be put in a sentence without any relator particle. It functions like an adverb. The counter system will be explained later on this lesson.

Another one is "de gozaimasu" which is practically same as "desu." The only difference is that "de gozaimasu" is very polite and it is used when formerly spoken by those who can use the language consistently in a polite way. It sounds funny unless spoken in the same speech level when using this polite form. You will often hear sales clerks of department stores in Tokyo speaking to their customers with the ending, "de gozaimasu."

Sochira no wa o-ikura desu ka.

"No" is not a possessive type of relator particle in this case. It functions as a pronoun equivalent to the one in English. Therefore, "sochira no" means "the one over there."

"No" indicates a belonging to somebody or something or somewhere.

Watakushi no	- mine
Yamada san no	- Mr. Yamada's
gakkoo no	- the one belonging to school
kurabu no	- the one belonging to the club
koko no/kochira no	- the one over here
soko no/sochira no	- the one over there
asoko no/achira no	- the one over that place

EXAMPLE: Tanaka san no kamera wa atarashii desu ga, Yamada san no wa furui desu.
(Mr. Tanaka's camera is new, but Mr. Yamada's is old.)

"O-ikura" means "How much." O- is prefix to make the word sound better or respectful of other party. In the presentation dialog, Hanako is a cutomer who is supposed to be superior to the sales clerk in the speech level, but nevertheless, she is using the respectful prefix. It gives a better feeling to the other party. Not only that, it indicates that the way she talks is polite.

In general, the more polite they get, the polite expressions they use in Japan no matter what level or position the other party may be in.

LET'S SPEAK JAPANESE

SPECIAL NOTE

There are two counting systems in Japanese - one the traditional Japanese system, and the other having been borrowed from the Chinese language. Beyond the number ten, the traditional Japanese system has virtually disappeared.

In general, the traditional system is used for counting things up to ten, and the Chinese system is used for counting things past ten. When certain classes of objects are counted in their totality the Chinese system is used, with appropriate classifiers, exclusively. Example:

| Hitotsu (wa) o-ikura desu ka. | - How much is one? |
| Go-hon kudasai. | - Please give me (a total of) five (slim & long things). |

There are some things that can be counted without classifiers, including children's age up to ten. In those cases, totals may be expressed in the Japanese system. The traditional Japanese numbers are never used with classifiers. Here are the two systems from one to ten.

Hito-tsu	ichi
futa-tsu	ni
mi-ttsu	san
yo-ttsu	shi, yon
itsu-tsu	go
mu-ttsu	roku
nana-tsu	shichi, nana
ya-ttsu	hachi
kokono-tsu	kyuu, ku
too	juu

The hyphens in the traditional Japanese list have nothing to do with pronunciation or spelling. The first part of the word is actually the numerical part; the -tsu or -ttsu is a sort of suffix.

The following are the numbers from 1-100. In all counting shi (four) is usually replaced by yo or yon, and shichi (seven) is often replaced by nana.

ichi	juu-roku	san-juu-ichi	yon-juu-roku	roku-juu-ichi
ni	juu-shichi	san-juu-ni	yon-juu-shichi	roku-juu-ni
san	juu-hachi	san-juu-san	yon-juu-hachi	roku-juu-san
shi, yon	juu-ku	san-juu-yon	yon-juu-ku	roku-juu-yon
go	ni-juu	san-juu-go	go-juu	roku-juu-go
roku	ni-juu-ichi	san-juu-roku	go-juu-ichi	roku-juu-roku
shichi	ni-juu-ni	san-juu-shichi	go-juu-ni	roku-juu-shichi
hachi	ni-juu-san	san-juu-hachi	go-juu-san	roku-juu-hachi
ku, kyuu	ni-juu-yon	san-juu-ku	go-juu-yon	roku-juu-ku
juu	ni-juu-go	yon-juu	go-juu-go	nana-juu
juu-ichi	ni-juu-roku	yon-juu-ichi	go-juu-roku	nana-juu-ichi
juu-ni	ni-juu shichi	yon-juu-ni	go-juu-shichi	nana-juu-ni
juu-san	ni-juu-hachi	yon-juu-san	go-juu-hachi	nana-juu-san
juu-yon	ni-juu-ku	yon-juu-yon	go-juu-ku	nana-juu-yon
juu-go	san-juu	yon-juu-go	roku-juu	nana-juu-go

nana-juu-roku	hachi-juu-roku	kyuu-juu-roku
nana-juu-nana	hachi-juu-nana	kyuu-juu-nana
nana-juu-hachi	hachi-juu-hachi	kyuu-juu-hachi
nana-juu-ku	hachi-juu-ku	kyuu-juu-kyuu
hachi-juu	kyuu-juu	hyaku
hachi-juu-ichi	kyuu-juu-ichi	
hachi-juu-ni	kyuu-juu-ni	
hachi-juu-san	kyuu-juu-san	
hachi-juu-yon	kyuu-juu-yon	
hachi-juu-go	kyuu-juu-go	

The classifiers are different, depending on items. Listed below are numeral classifiers and category/items.

Numeral Classifier	Category/Items	
en	currency	yen
doru	currency	dollar
sento	currency	cent
mai	thin, flat:	paper, sheet, shirt, etc.
dai	machine:	automobile, typewriter, etc.
kai	floor:	floors of department store, building, etc.
ki		airplane, missle, etc.
satsu	book:	magazine, books, etc.
hon	slim, long:	pencil, chalk, bamboo pole, tree, etc. (Depending on preceding numeral, the pronunciation sometimes changes to -pon or -bon. Example: i-ppon, san-bon)
sai	age	
hiki	animal & fish	cat, dog, monkey, fish (Depending on preceeding numeral, the pronunciation changes to -piki or -biki like i-ppiki, san-biki, etc.)
too	animal:	horse, cow, camel, etc.
nin	human being:	student, teacher, children, etc. ("One person" and "two persons" are the only exceptions: hitori and futari, both traditional words that refuse to be replaced by "ichi-nin" and "ni-nin.")
soku	foot ware:	shoes, socks, boots, slippers, etc.

LET'S SPEAK JAPANESE

- chaku   apparel: dress, suit, etc.
- ji   time: o'clock
- fun   time: minute (Depending on preceding numerals, the pronunciation changes to pun or fun like i-ppun and ni-fun.)

- byoo   time: second
- jikan   time: hour (s)

SHORT DIALOGS - MEMORIZE

DIALOG 1:

A: Irasshaimase.
B: Kono zasshi wa issatsu o-ikura desu ka.
A: Kore de gozaimasu ka. Kore wa issatsu hachi-juu-ha-ssento de gozaimasu.
B: Soo desu ka. Dewa, sore o issatsu kudasai.
A; Hai, kashikomarimashita.

DIALOG 2:

A: Irasshaimase.
B: Kono buhin wa o-ikura desu ka.
A: Kore de gozaimasu ka. Kore wa hitotsu san-doru-go-ju-ssento de gozaimasu.
B: Soo desu ka. Dewa, sore o hitotsu kudasai.
A: Hai, kashikomarimashita

DRILLS

QUESTIONS AND ANSWERS

1. Kono kutsu wa i-ssoku o-ikura desu ka.   Sore wa i-ssoku juu-yon doru de gozaimasu.
2. Kono terebi wa ichi-dai o-ikura desu ka.   Sore wa ichi-dai kyuu-juu hachi doru de gozaimasu.
3. Kono fuku wa i-cchaku o-ikura desu ka.   Sore wa i-cchaku roku-juu kyuu doru de gozaimasu.
4. Kono pen wa i-ppon o-ikura desu ka.   Sore wa i-ppon ni doru nana-juu go sento de gozaimasu.

TRANSFORMATION DRILLS

Change the "de gozaimasu" to "desu" form.

1. Sore wa go sento de gozaimasu.   Sore wa go sento desu.
2. Sore wa juu doru de gozaimasu.   Sore wa juu doru desu.
3. Sore wa san-juu-go doru de gozaimasu.   Sore wa san-juu-go doru desu.
4. Sore wa hyaku doru de gozaimasu.   Sore wa hyaku doru desu.

5. Watakushi wa Tamura de gozaimasu.   Watakushi wa Tamura desu.
6. Ano kata wa sensei de gozaimasu.   Ano kata wa sensei desu.
7. Koko wa jimusho de gozaimasu.   Koko wa jimusho desu.
8. Are wa Tookyoo Tawaa de gozaimasu.   Are wa Tookyoo Tawaa desu.

EXERCISES

1. Match the following numeral classifiers with proper items. Fill in each blank with a proper letter from the Groups A, B and C.

	A	B	C
1. kyuu-mai	( )	( )	( )
2. hachi-nin	( )	( )	( )
3. yon-dai	( )	( )	( )
4. go-hon	( )	( )	( )
5. roku-satsu	( )	( )	( )

A	B	C
A. automobile	A. book	A. children
B. dictionary	B. typewriter	B. tree
C. shirt	C. fountain-pen	C. plate
D. bottle	D. paper	D. sewing machine
E. student	E. men	E. magazine

2. Express the following sentences in Japanese.

   1. How much is this apple per pound?
   2. It is one dollar per lb.
   3. How much is the one over there?
   4. The one over here is one dollar and twenty cents.

3. Make a dialog based on the following situation.

   Miss Kathy stops by a jewelry store in Tokyo, where she is going to buy a watch at a decent price. When she enters the store, a sales clerk greets her for welcome and responds to Kathy's inquiry. Kathy finally decides to buy one near her.

USEFUL EXPRESSIONS (1)

Ohayoo gozaimasu.	Good morning.
Kon'nichi wa.	Good day. Good afternoon.
Kon'ban wa.	Good evening.
Sayoonara.	Good bye.
Oyasumi-nasai.	Good night.
O-genki desu ka.	How are you? (Lit. Are you fine?)
Hai, okage-sama de, genki desu.	Yes, thanks for asking, I'm fine. (Lit. Yes, thanks to you, I'm fine.)
Anata wa.	And you?
Shitsurei shimasu.	Excuse me. (when leaving.)
Hai, doozo.	Yes, please. (Please go ahead.)
O-daiji ni.	Be careful. Please take care.
Ki o tsukete.	(Lit. Be alert.)
Yoku dekimashita.	You did very well.
Onegai shimasu.	Please. (Do me a favor.)
Doozo.	Please. (Go ahead.)
Gomen kudasai.	Please excuse me. (When visiting somebody's home and knocking at the door.)
Gomen nasai	Please excuse me. Pardon me. (When apologizing.)
Doomo sumimasen.	I am sorry. Thank you. (People often use this expression instead of "Arigatoo gozaimasu.)
Arigatoo gozaimasu.	Thank you. (Present favors.)
Arigatoo gozaimashita.	Thank you. (Past favors.)
Doo itashimashite.	You are welcome. Not at all. Don't mention it. (Appropriate answer to arigatoo, sumimasen, etc.)
Koohii o kudasai.	Coffee, please. (Lit. Please give me coffee.)
Kashikomarimashita.	Certainly. At your service. I understand. (Often in reply to o-negaishimasu, and other requests for favors, help, etc.)
Go-shinsetsu ni, doomo, arigatoo gozaimasu.	Thank you very much for having been very kind to me.
Gokuroo-sama deshita.	Thanks for your trouble. You have been a lot of trouble. (Working hard.)
O-saki ni, shitsurei shimasu.	Excuse me. I'm going first.
O-kamai-naku.	Please don't bother.
O-jama shimasu.	I'm going to bother you.
Doomo o-jama shimashita.	I've been a bother.
Soo desu.	That's right.

USEFUL EXPRESSIONS (2)

Soo desu ne.	That's right, isn't it?
Soo desu nee . . .	Well, let's see . . .
Soo ja arimasen.	That's not right.
Iie, chigaimasu.	No, it's different.
Iie, tondemo arimasen.	No, never.
Maido arigatoo gozaimasu.	Thank you everytime (for your patronage).
Shooshoo o-machi kudasai. kudasaimase.	Please wait a moment.
Chotto matte kudasai.	Please wait.
O-matase itashimashita.	I am sorry to have kept you waiting.
Mata doozo.	Please come again.
Mata oide kudasai.	Please come again.
Shibaraku deshita.	It has been a long time to see you.
Shibaraku desu nee.	It's a long time to see you, isn't it?
Hisashi buri desu nee.	It's a long time to see you, isn't it?
O-sewa ni narimashita.	Thank you for your assistance. (Lit. I have been your charge.)
Zannen desu nee.	That's unfortunate!
O-ki-no-doku desu.	I am sorry to hear it.
Sore wa ikemasen nee.	That shouldn't be! That's too bad!
Tadaima.	I'm home.
Okaerinasai.	Welcome back.
Itte mairimasu.	Goodbye (when leaving home or office for a business trip. (Lit. I'm going and coming.)
Itte irasshai.	Goodbye (To the one leaving home or office. Lit. Go and come!)
Doo shimashita ka.	What happened?
Shikata ga arimasen.	There's nothing that can be done.
Shiyoo ga arimasen.	There's nothing that can be done.
Yamu o emasen.	There's nothing that can be done.
Nodo ga kawakimashita.	I'm thirsty.
Nodo ga karakara desu.	I'm thirsty (to the utmost).
O-naka ga sukimashita.	I'm hungry.
O-naka ga pekopeko desu.	I'm hungry (to the utmost).
O-mizu o kudasai.	Please give me some water.
Sukoshi dake kudasai.	Just a little please.
Tsukarete imasu.	I'm tired.
O-tsukare deshoo.	You must be tired.

LET'S SPEAK JAPANESE

USEFUL EXPRESSIONS (3)

Yokatta desu ka.	Was it good? How did you like it?
Yokatta desu.	It was good. I liked it.
Sore wa yokatta desu.	I'm glad that you liked it.
Omoshirokatta desu ka.	Was it fun? Did you enjoy it?
Omoshirokatta desu.	It was fun. I enjoyed it.
Choodo ii desu.	It's just right.
Go-ran nasai.	Look. See. Observe.
Go-ran ni narimashita ka.	Did you see (it)?
Iie, mada desu.	No, not yet.
Go-zonji desu ka.	Do you know (him, her, it, a fact)?
Iie, shirimasen.	No, I don't know.
Iie, zonjimasen.	No, I don't know. (polite)
O-kyaku-san desu.	It's a guest (guests).
O-kyaku-sama desu.	It's a guest (polite).
Donata desu ka.	Who is it?
Go-busata shimashita.	Pardon my silence.
Senjitsu wa doomo arigatoo gozaimashita.	Thank you for your kindness the other day.
Doozo o-hairi kudasai.	Please come in.
O-rikoo-san desu nee.	What a smart child.
Doozo meshi-agatte kudasai.	Please help yourself (at mealtimes).
Doozo o-meshiagari kudasai.	Please help yourself (polite).
Go-enryo naku, doozo . . .	Don't be reluctant, please . . .
Itadakimasu.	I will accept it.
Go-chisoo sama deshita.	It was a feast.
O-dekake desu ka.	Are you going (somewhere)?
Ee, chotto soko made.	Yes, I am going there for a while.
O-kaimono desu ka.	Are you going for shopping?
Ee, chotto depaato made.	Yes, I am going (as far as) to the department store.
Ima nan-ji desu ka.	What time is it now?
Ku-ji desu.	It's nine o'clock.
Ku-ji han desu.	It's half past nine.
Kyoo wa nan-yoobi desu ka.	What day of the week is it today?
Nichi-yoobi desu.	It's Sunday.
Getsu-yoobi desu.	It's Monday.
Ka-yoobi desu.	It's Tuesday.
Sui-yoobi desu.	It's Wednesday.
Moku-yoobi desu.	It's Thursday.
Kin-yoobi desu.	It's Friday.
Do-yoobi desu.	It's Saturday.
Dare ga kimasu ka.	Who is coming?
Donata ga kimasu ka.	Who is coming?
Dare mo kimasen yo.	Nobody is coming to be sure.
Dare mo ikimasen.	Nobody is going.
Dare mo tabemasen.	Nobody eats.

CHART OF ADJECTIVES

takai	-high, expensive	hiratai	-flat
yasui	-cheap	shitashii	-familiar, close, intimate
hikui	-low	hiroi	-spacious, wide
oishii	-delicious	semai	-narrow, small
mazui	-distasteful	abunai	-dangerous, risky
tooi	-far	nagai	-long
chikai	-close, near	mijikai	-short
ookii (dekkai)	-big, large	wakai	-young
chiisai	-small	hidoi	-terrible
utsukushii	-beautiful	tadashii	-right
kitanai	-dirty	arai	-rough
kitsui	-tight	osoroshii	-fearful, dreadful
yurui	-loose	kowai*	-fearful, frightful
kibishii	-strict	kowai*	-tough, wiry
yasashii*	-kind, gentle	hageshii	-violent, furious
katai	-hard	iyashii	-greedy, mean, vulgar
yawarakai	-soft	iyarashii	-disgusting, obscene
ii (yoi) (yoroshii)	-good	minikui	-ugly
warui	-bad	hayai	-early, fast
akarui	-light, bright	osoi	-slow
kurai	-dark	isogashii	-busy
kagayakashii	-brilliant	sesekomashii	-narrow & crowded
omoshiroi	-interesting	sugoi	-terrific
tsumaranai	-uninteresting	yakamashii	-noisy
okashii	-funny	sawagashii	-noisy
fukai	-deep	soozooshii	-noisy
asai	-shallow	nemui	-sleepy
tsuyoi	-strong	mazushii	-poor
yowai	-weak	aoi	-blue
chikarazuyoi	-powerful, reassuring	kuroi	-black
muzukashii	-difficult	shiroi	-white
yasashii*	-easy	akai	-red
itai	-sore, hurt	kiiroi	-yellow
hosoi	-thin, slender	chairoi	-brown
futoi	-big, thick, burly	shikakui	-square
atsui*	-hot	marui	-round
samui	-cold (atmosphere)	tsurai	-hard, painful, trying
tsumetai	-cold (touch)	ichijirushii	-remarkable, outstanding
atatakai	-warm	kanbashii	-fragrant, favorable
suzushii	-cool	inshoobukai	-impressive
mushi-atsui	-hot and stuffy, sultry	sugasugashii	-refreshing, bracing

nurui	-luke warm	natsukashii	-dear, longed-for
omoi	-heavy	koishii	-sweet, beloved, affectionate
karui	-light	mabushii	-dazzling, blinding
sukunai	-little	urayamashii	-envious
ooi	-plenty	ureshii	-happy
atarashii	-new	kanashii	-sad
furui	-old	sabishii	-lonely
atsui*	-thick	wabishii	-wretched, lonesome
usui	-thin	subarashii	-wonderful
koi	-dark (color) thick, heavy (tea)	chuuibukai karugarushii	-careful -thoughtless, imprudent
noroi	-slow	memeshii	-womanish, effeminate
munashii	-empty, void	uiuishii	-innocent, naive
zuuzuushii	-impudent, cool shameless	mizumizushii	-young and fresh
zurui	-shrewd	nozomashii	-desirable, advisable
itamashii	-sad, piteous touching	hoshii	-want, need
ikagawashii	-unreliable, doubtful	ayashii	-doubtful, dubious
ikameshii	-solemn, majectic	ibukashii	-doubtful, dubious
awatadashii	-busy, bustling	kokoroyoi	-pleasant, agreeable
misuborashii	-shabby, poor	kusuguttai	-ticklish
narenareshii	-familiar, unceremonious	osanai	-infant, young
itaitashii	-pitiful, touching	shibui	-astringent, puckery
satoi	-clever, intelligent	hitoshii	-equal
kashikoi	-wise	tanomoshii	-reliable, hopeful
kuyashii	-regrettable, mortifying	tegowai	-stiff, tough
iyarashii	-disgusting, obscene	kurushii	-painful, afflicting
takumashii	-stout, sturdy	itowashii	-abominable
tsutsumashii	-modest, reserved	nigai	-bitter
isamashii	-brave	karai	-hot
ririshii	-gallant & forbidding, dignified	amai	-sweet
yuyushii	-serious, grave	shoppai	-salty
fusawashii	-suitable, becoming	suppai	-sour
hohoemashii	-heartening, pleasant	kanbashii	-sweet, fragrant, favorable
modokashii	-irritating	koobashii	-sweet

jirettai	-irritating	susamajii	-terrible, tremendous
hagayui	-irritating	uruwashii	-beautiful, lovely
omowashii	-satisfactory, desirable	koogooshii	-divine, godly
kizewashii	-restless	kusai	-ill-smelling, stinking
atsukamashii	-shameless, brazen (faced)	imaimashii	-vexing, annoying
okogamashii	-presumptious	mimeyoi	-well-favored
menbokunai	-be ashamed	kawaii	-cute
hazukashii	-be ashamed, bashful	yasuppoi	-cheapish
yurui	-loose, lenient	namidappoi	-easily moved
kayui	-itchy	okorippoi	-excitable, irritable
machidooshii	-(feel) impatient	arappoi	-wild, violent
moroi	-fragile	kizappoi	-affected
namida-moroi	-lachrymose, easily moved	iroppoi	-amorous, erotic
namida-gumashii	-tearful, pathetic	kodomoppoi	-childish
osore-ooi	-gracious, august	omo'omoshii	-solemn, grave
uya'uyashii	-respectful, reverent	darashinai	-sloppy
kimari-warui	-awkward	uttooshii	-gloomy, depressing
memagurushii	-dizzy, dazing	kayowai	-frail, delicate
bakabakashii	-absurd, ridiculous	hakabakashii	-rapid, satisfactory

LET'S SPEAK JAPANESE

PATTERN SENTENCES OF ADJECTIVES

Kono tochi wa takai desu.	This land is expensive.
Kono tochi wa takai deshoo.	This land must be expensive.
Sono tochi mo takai shi, kono tochi mo takai desu nee.	That land is expensive and this land is expensive, too, isn't it!
Ima kono kabu wa takaku arimasen.	This stock is not expensive now.
Bukka wa kyonen takakatta desu.	The commodities were expensive last year.
Ototoshi wa sonna ni takaku arimasen deshita.	They were not that much expensive the year before last.
Sore wa takakute mo kaitai desu.	Even if it is expensive, I want to buy it.
Ringo wa takakute mo, banana wa yasui desu.	Even though the apple is expensive, banana is cheap.
Kyaderakku wa Toyota yori takai desu.	Cadillac is more expensive than Toyota.
Kore ga ichiban takai desu.	This is the most expensive.
Ima wa niku ga takakute, amari kaimasen.	Meat is expensive now and I don't buy it so much.
Amari takakereba, hoshiku arimasen.	If it is too expensive, I don't want it.
Amari takakute wa, hoshiku arimasen.	If it is too expensive, I don't want it.
Takaku nakereba narimasen.	It's got to be expensive.
Takaku nakereba, kaimasu.	If it is not expensive, I'll buy it.
Takaku nakute mo, kore wa ii shinamono desu.	Even though it is not expensive, this is good merchandise.
Takakattara, kaimasen.	If it is expensive, I won't buy it.
Takaku nakattara, kaimasu.	If it is not expensive, I'll buy it.
Takai toki wa,- - -*	When it is expensive, - - -*
Takai baai wa, - - -*	In case that it is expensive, - - -*
Takai node, - - -*	Since it is expensive, - - -*
Takai kara, - - -*	Because it is expensive, - - -*
Takai no ni, - - -*	In spite of being expensive, - - -*
Takai ni mo kakawarazu, - - -*	In spite of being expensive, - - -*
Takai desu ga, - - -*	It is expensive, but - -*
Taka-sugimasu.	It is too expensive.*

CHART OF NOUN-ADJECTIVES

kirei	-pretty	taiman	-lazy
suki	-likeable	namaiki	-presumptuous, saucy
kirai	-dislikeable	taira	-plain, flat
benri	-convenient	heiki	-calm, cool (attitude)
fuben	-inconvenient	taihen	-terrible, awful
yuumei	-famous	mijime	-pitiful
shizuka	-quiet	reisei	-indifferent
rippa	-splendid, fine	ubu	-naive
genki	-lively, healthy	hikaeme	-moderate, temperate
tokutei	-particular	kiza	-affected, disagreeable
hitsuyoo	-necessary, needy	yuruyaka	-loose, easy, lax
omo	-main	nadaraka	-gently-sloping
iroiro	-various	nodoka	-tranquil, calm peaceful
suteki	-wonderful	hikyoo	-cowardly, mean, unfair
kanshin	-admirable	azayaka	-vivid, clear
yuuryoku	-powerful, influential	hade	-gay, showy, flashy
kokkei	-funny	jimi	-plain, simple, modest
takumi	-skillful, ingenious	koomyoo	-tactful, skillful
joobu	-strong, sturdy	kimyoo	-strange
joozu	-skillful, good	fushigi	-strange
kawaisoo	-sorry, pitiful	kandai	-generous, lenient
shinkoku	-serious	koodai	-spacious, broad
juuyoo	-important	idai	-great
taisetsu	-important	heitan	-plain (place)
juudai	-important	muri	-unreasonable
kantan	-simple	muda	-useless, waste
tanjun	-simple-hearted	onwa	-mild, gentle
yooi	-easy	baka	-foolish, crazy
kenzen	-sound	iya	-disagreeable
kimagure	-capricious, changeable	majime	-serious
shitsurei	-impolite	mu-funbetsu	-indiscreet, thoughtless
teinei	-polite	mucha	-absurd, unreasonable
meikaku	-precise	muchi	-ignorant
kyasha	-delicate, slender	fu-koohei	-unfair, unjust
ganjoo	-solid, firm, stout	shinsetsu	-kind
heta	-unskilled	fu-shinsetsu	-unkind
yakkai	-troublesome, annoying	ijiwaru	-mean, nasty
nigate	-undesirable	kindai-teki	-modern
kichoomen	-methodical, neat	shakai-teki	-socialistic
kichoo	-precious, invaluable	gutai-teki	-concrete

LET'S SPEAK JAPANESE

kisaku	-open-hearted	kyakkan-teki	-objective
joohin	-elegant	kojin-teki	-individual
seidai	-prosperous, grand	kihon-teki	-basic
sasai	-trivial	gendai-teki	-contemporary
heibon	-common, ordinary	sekkyoku-teki	-positive
raku	-comfortable, easy	shookyoku-teki	-negative, passive
shinsen	-fresh	hoshu-teki	-conservative
samazama	-various	daihyoo-teki	-representative
keisotsu	-hasty, rush	ichiji-teki	-temporary
aware	-miserable	riko-teki	-selfish
migoto	-nice, beautiful	ippan-teki	-general
yutaka	-rich	miryoku-teki	-attractive
hoofu	-abundant, rich		

PATTERN SENTENCES OF NOUN-ADJECTIVES

Kono hana wa kirei desu.	This flower is pretty.
Sono hana wa kirei deshoo.	That flower must be pretty.
Kono hana mo kirei da shi, sono hana mo kirei desu nee.	This flower is pretty and that flower is pretty, too, isn't it!
Kono hana wa kirei ja arimasen.	This flower is not pretty.
Sono hana wa kirei deshita.	That flower was pretty.
Sono hana wa son'na ni kirei ja arimasen deshita.	That flower was not that much pretty.
Sore wa kirei de mo, kaimasen.	Even if it is pretty, I don't buy it.
Koko wa kirei de mo, soko wa kitanai desu.	Even though this (here) is pretty, it's dirty down there.
Kono machi wa sono machi yori kirei desu.	This town is prettier than that town.
Kore ga ichiban kirei desu.	This is the prettiest.
Nihon wa aki ga kirei de, maitoshi ikimasu.	The autumn is pretty in Japan, and I go there every year.
Soko ga kirei nara, zehi ikitai desu.	If it's pretty over there, I want to go by all means.
Kirei de nakereba, kaimasen.	If it's not pretty, I won't buy it.
Kirei de nakutemo, ii tokoro desu yo.	Even though it is not pretty, it's a good place.
Kirei dattara, kaimasu.	If it is pretty, I will buy it.
Kirei de nakattara, kaimasen.	If it is not pretty, I won't buy it.
* Kirei na toki, - - -	When it is pretty, - - -
* Kirei na baai wa, - - -	In case that is pretty, - - -
* Kirei na node, - - -	Since it is pretty, - - -
* Kirei da kara, - - - (Kirei desu kara,)	Because it is pretty, - - -
* Kirei na noni, - - -	In spite of being pretty, - - -
* Kirei na noni mo kakawarazu, - - -	In spite of being pretty, - - -
* Kirei desu ga, - - -	It is pretty, but - - -
* Kirei-sugimasu.	It is too pretty.

LET'S SPEAK JAPANESE

VERB CHART

Plain Present Future (Modifies nouns, can be followed by no desu)	Nominal Base (+ masu masen mashita mashoo nasai, tai nagara, etc.)	Non-Final (Te-form) (+ imasu kudasai kara mo morau, etc.)	Plain Past (Modifies nouns, can be followed by no desu)	Plain Negative (can be followed by no desu)
Vowel Verbs				
taberu	tabe	tabete	tabeta	tabenai
miru	mi	mite	mita	minai
oshieru	oshie	oshiete	oshieta	oshienai
kangaeru	kangae	kangaete	kangaeta	kangaenai
ageru	age	agete	ageta	agenai
tomeru	tome	tomete	tometa	tomenai
shiraseru	shirase	shirasete	shiraseta	shirasenai
hirogeru	hiroge	hirogete	hirogeta	hirogenai
mukaeru	mukae	mukaete	mukaeta	mukaenai
kimeru	kime	kimete	kimeta	kimenai
umareru	umare	umarete	umareta	umarenai
kuraberu	kurabe	kurabete	kurabeta	kurabenai
yogoreru	yogore	yogorete	yogoreta	yogorenai
tsubureru	tsubure	tsuburete	tsubureta	tsuburenai
hajimeru	hajime	hajimete	hajimeta	hajimenai
Consonant Verbs				
iku	iki	itte	itta	ikanai
asobu	asobi	asonde	asonda	asobanai
yomu	yomi	yonde	yonda	yomanai
nomu	nomi	nonde	nonda	nomanai
kiku	kiki	kiite	kiita	kikanai
kaku	kaki	kaite	kaita	kakanai
isogu	isogi	isoide	isoida	isoganai
hanasu	hanashi	hanashite	hanashita	hanasanai
wakaru	wakari	wakatte	wakatta	wakaranai
kau	kai	katte	katta	kawanai
uru	uri	utte	utta	uranai
kasu	kashi	kashite	kashita	kasanai
yobu	yobi	yonde	yonda	yobanai
hakobu	hakobi	hakonde	hakonda	hakobanai
nozomu	nozomi	nozonde	nozonda	nozomanai
Irregular Verbs				
kuru	ki	kite	kita	konai
suru	shi	shite	shita	shinai

NOTE: Hundreds of action verbs can be made up with the irregular verb "suru," such as: benkyoo suru, kenkyuu suru, ryokoo suru, shitsumon suru, gorufu (& all sports) suru, undoo suru, ryoori suru, kooshoo suru, etc.

PATTERN SENTENCES OF VERBS
(1) VOWEL VERBS

tabe-ru (-masu)	(I) will eat (contemplate).
tabe-ta (-mashita)	(I) ate.
tabe-nasai.	Eat!
tabe-tai desu.	I want to eat.
tabe-taku arimasen.	I don't want to eat.
tabe-takatta desu.	I wanted to eat.
tabe-taku arimasen deshita.	I didn't want to eat.
tabe-takattara . . .	If (you) want(ed) to eat . . .
tabe-takereba . . .	If (you) want to eat . . .
tabe-nai desu.	(I) will not eat.
tabe-masen.	(I) will not eat.
tabe-nakatta desu.	(I) did't eat.
tabe-naide kudasai.	Please don't eat.
tabe-nakattara . . .	If (you) had not eaten . . .
tabe-nakereba . . .	If (you) don't eat . . .
tabe-nakereba narimasen.	(You) must eat.
tabe-tara . . .	If (I) ate . . .
tabe-reba . . .	If (I) eat . . .
tabe-mashoo.	Let's eat.
tabete mo ii desu.	You may eat.
tabete wa ikemasen.	You must not eat.
tabeta hoo ga ii desu.	You had better eat.
tabeta kamo shiremasen	(He) may have eaten it.
taberu kamo shiremasen.	(He) may eat it.
taberu tsumori desu.	I intend to eat it.
taberu hazu desu.	(He) is supposed to eat it.
taberu dake desu.	(I) only eat it.
taberu toki . . .	When (I) eat . . .
taberu baai . . .	In case (I) eat . . .
taberu node . . .	Since (I) eat . . .
taberu kara . . .	Because (I) eat . . .
taberu noni . . .	in spite of eating . . .
taberu noni mo kakawarazu . . .	in spite of eating . . .
taberu no ni . . .	to eat (infinitive function)
taberu to . . .	If (you) eat, . . .
taberu tame ni . . .	in order to eat . . .
tabe-sugimasu.	(You) overeat.
tabete kara, . . .	After (I) eat, . . .
tabete mo . . .	Even though (I) eat, . . .
tabe-nagara . . .	While eating . . .
tabete kudasai.	Please eat.

PATTERN SENTENCES OF VERBS
(2) CONSONANT VERBS

ik-u (-imasu)	(I) will go (contemplate).
itta (ikimashita)	(I) went.
iki-nasai.	Go!
iki-tai desu.	I want to go.
iki-taku arimasen.	I don't want to go.
iki-takatta desu.	I wanted to go.
iki-taku arimasen deshita.	I didn't want to go.
iki-takattara.	If (you) want(ed) to go . . .
iki-takereba . . .	If (you) want to go . . .
ika-nai desu.	(I) will not go.
iki masen.	(I) will not go.
ika-nakatta desu.	(I) didn't go.
ika-naide kudasai.	Please don't go.
ika-nakattara . . .	If (you) had not gone . . .
ika-nakereba . . .	If (you) don't go . . .
ika-nakereba narimasen.	(You) must go.
ittara . . .	If (I) went . . .
ikeba . . .	If (I) go . . .
iki-mashoo.	Let's go.
itte mo ii desu.	You may go.
itte wa ikemasen.	You must not go.
itta hoo ga ii desu.	You had better go.
itta kamo shiremasen.	(He) may have gone.
iku kamo shiremasen.	(He) may go.
iku tsumori desu.	I intend to go.
iku hazu desu.	(He) is supposed to go.
iku dake desu.	(I) only go.
iku toki, . . .	When (I) go, . . .
iku baai, . . .	In case (I) go, . . .
iku node, . . .	Since (I) go, . . .
iku kara, . . .	Because (I) go, . . .
iku noni . . .	in spite of going . . .
iku noni mo kakawarazu . . .	in spite of going . . .
iku no ni . . .	to go (infinitive function)
iku to, . . .	If (you) go, . . .
iku tame ni . . .	in order to go . . .
iki-sugimasu.	(You) go too much.

itte kara . . .   After (I) go, . . .
itte mo, . . .   Even though (I) go, . . .
iki-nagara . . .   While going . . .

itte kudasai.   Please go.

LET'S SPEAK JAPANESE

PATTERN SENTENCES OF VERBS
(3) IRREGULAR VERBS - KURU

ku-ru (ki-masu)	(I) will come (contemplate).
ki-ta (ki-mashita)	(He) came.
ki-nasai.	Come!
ki-tai desu.	I want to come.
ki-taku arimasen.	I don't want to come.
ki-takatta desu.	I wanted to come.
ki-taku arimasen deshita.	I didn't want to come.
ki-takattara . . .	If (you) want(ed) to come . .
ki-takereba . . .	If (you) want to come . . .
ko-nai desu.	(He) won't come.
ki-masen.	(He) won't come.
ko-nakatta desu.	(He) didn't come.
ko-naide kudasai.	Please don't come.
ko-nakattara . . .	If (he) had not come . . .
ko-nakereba . . .	If (he) doesn't come . . .
ko-nakereba narimasen.	(You) must come.
ki-tara, . . .	If (he) came, . . .
ku-reba . . .	If (he) comes . . .
ki-mashoo.	Let's come.
kite mo ii desu.	You may come.
kite wa ikemasen.	You must not come.
kita hoo ga ii desu.	You had better come.
kita kamo shiremasen.	(He) may have come.
kuru kamo shiremasen.	(He) may come.
kuru tsumori desu.	I intend to come.
kuru hazu desu.	(He) is supposed to come.
kuru dake desu.	(I) only come.
kuru toki, . . .	When (I) come, . . .
kuru baai, . . .	In case (I) come, . . .
kuru node, . . .	Since (I) come, . . .
kuru kara, . . .	Because (I) come, . . .
kuru noni . . .	in spite of coming . . .
kuro noni mo kakawarazu . . .	in spite of coming . . .
kuru no ni . . .	to come (infinitive function)
kuru to . . .	If (you) come, . . .
kuru tame ni . . .	in order to come . . .
ki-sugimasu.	(You) come too much.
kite kara, . . .	After (he) comes, . . .
kite mo, . . .	Even though (he) comes, . . .
ki-nagara . . .	While coming . . .
kite kudasai.	Please come.

IRREGULAR VERBS - SURU

benkyoo suru	study
benkyoo su-ru (shi-masu).	(I) will study (comtemplate).
benkyoo shi-ta (shi-mashita).	(I) studied.
benkyoo shi-nasai.	Study!
benkyoo shi-tai desu.	I want to study.
benkyoo shi-taku arimasen.	I don't want to study.
benkyoo shi-takatta desu.	I wanted to study.
benkyoo shi-taku arimasen deshita.	I didn't want to study.
benkyoo shi-takattara . . .	If (you) want(ed) to study . . .
benkyoo shi-takereba . . .	If (you) want to study . . .
benkyoo shi-nai desu.	(He) won't study.
benkyoo shi-masen.	(He) won't study.
benkyoo shi-nakatta desu.	(He) did't study.
benkyoo shi-naide kudasai.	Please don't study.
benkyoo shi-nakattara . . .	If (you) had not studied . . .
benkyoo shi-nakereba . . .	If (you) don't study . . .
benkyoo shi-nakereba narimasen.	(You) must study.
benkyoo shi-tara, . . .	If (you) studied, . . .
benkyoo su-reba, . . .	If (you) study, . . .
benkyoo shi-mashoo.	Let's study.
benkyoo shite mo ii desu.	You may study.
benkyoo shite wa ikemasen.	You must not study.
benkyoo shita hoo ga ii desu.	You had better study.
benkyoo shita kamo shiremasen.	(He) may have studied.
benkyoo suru kamo shiremasen.	(He) may study.
benkyoo suru tsumori desu.	I intend to study.
benkyoo suru hazu desu.	(He) is supposed to study.
benkyoo suru dake desu.	(I) only study.
benkyoo suru toki, . . .	When (I) study, . . .
benkyoo suru baai, . . .	In case (I) study, . . .
benkyoo suru node, . . .	Since (I) study, . . .
benkyoo suru kara, . . .	Because (I) study, . . .
benkyoo suru noni . . .	In spite of studying . . .
benkyoo suru noni mo kakawarazu . . .	In spite of studying . . .
benkyoo suru no ni . . .	To study (infinitive function)
benkyoo suru to, . . .	If (you) study, . . .
benkyoo suru tame ni . . .	In order to study . . .
benkyoo shi-sugimasu.	(You) study too much.
benkyoo shite kara, . . .	After (I) study, . . .
benkyoo shite mo, . . .	Even though (I) study, . . .
benkyoo shi-nagara . . .	While studying . . .
benkyoo shite kudasai.	Please study.